FRIGID A VERY COLD CASE

THE 1991 UNITED BANK ROBBERY

KIMBERLI ROESSING ANDERSON

FRIGID

A VERY COLD CASE

The 1991 United Bank Robbery
By Kimberli Roessing-Anderson

For Brian
Who gives me space and time to write

"A jury consists of twelve persons chosen to decide who has the better lawyer"
Robert Frost

ACKNOWLEDGMENTS

Adams County Records Department
   Ahsan Ali
   Ancestry.com
   Bill Buckley (prosecutor on the King Case)
   Cody McCarthy (brother of Scott McCarthy)
   Court TV Archives
   Daily Sentinel, Grand Junction, 1991, 1992
   David Barranco (eye-witness and survivor)
   David Twist (eye-witness and survivor)
   DeLila Wilson (VHS tapes)
   Denver County Court Records Department
   Denver Post
   Denver Public Library
   Dorothy Stevenson (juror)
   Ed Arnhold (ammunition and firearms)
   Frank "Pancho" Redman
   J. Brian Anderson (photography)
   Jack A. Rushin (juror)
   James Prado (security supervisor)
   Jennifer Rios (wife of Scott McCarthy)

Kaila Roessing Anderson

Kat Klingberg (illustrator)

Maria Christian (eye-witness and survivor)

Myra King (sister of Jim King)

Newspaper Archives.com

Newspaper.com

People Magazine

Phil Goodstein "Murders in the Bank Vault"

Reza Jalini (juror)

Rocky Mountain News, 1991, 1992

Scott Robinson (attorney for James King)

Thurston "Bird" Birdwell

Thomas R. Brunn (juror)

Tom King (brother of James King)

Thomas Tatalanski (security manager)

Tawnya Wilson (sister of Todd Wilson)

Zillow

PREFACE

While writing this book, I have met some amazing, resilient people. I conducted over 25 interviews of jurors, eye-witnesses, prosecutors, defense attorneys, family members and friends, members of the King family, and employees of the bank. I watched 84 hours of trial tape from the case of Colorado versus James W. King in 1992. I have read about 400 news articles from all over the country about this case, and I have read 1000 pages of trial motions and transcripts. I have reviewed hundreds of bank documents. I have become a student of the case. I re-read the 1997 book about the case, Murders in the Bank Vault, written by Walter Gerash and Phil Goodstein. I found the VHS tapes of the trial crucial to the understanding of what happened and how the jury could have reached its decision.

For a while, I took up residence at the City and County Building in Denver. I also staked out my own desk at the Denver Public Library. I had painful conversations with the families that left me in tears. I have laughed with the people I interviewed and cried with them, depending on the story and time. What started as a story idea became a mission for justice. These four young bank guards who were murdered on Father's Day in 1991 have become my brothers. James King is dead, but the case doesn't have to be. Items in evidence could still be tested for DNA. The families and victims, in this case, deserve justice. The six survivors deserve justice. This cold case needs to be worked again with fresh eyes and new investigators. DNA testing needs to be utilized.

INTRODUCTION

He was traveling quickly and quietly through the maze of tunnels. He wiped the blood from himself. He had known this place before. He knew the smell of the damp and the gray of the color. The smell of mildew filled his nostrils. He was a little out of breath. The adrenaline was carrying him. Almost to the guard station. Would he kill more? Would they recognize him? The felt hat seemed silly but necessary all the same. The sunglasses were a nuisance in the dark tunnels, yet they hid the color and shape of his eyes. Would his attempts at a disguise be enough? Would he have to kill everyone?

In a few moments, gunshots would ring out, and a cloud of gun smoke would fill the air. The sight of bright red blood would splatter on the white flooring. The brightly lit room would draw a sharp contrast between the red and the white. Lifeless bodies. The metallic smell from the blood overwhelmed him. He was nauseated and had to turn away and cover his mouth and nose. He gagged. Eighteen rounds had been fired. Seventeen into four bank guards whose lifeless eyes now looked at nothing. Live video monitors showed different parts of the bank on the walls. It was time to get to work and move on. He had rehearsed this in his mind a thousand times.

Each step was methodical. Take a tape, take a step, wipe down a surface, take a step. No fingerprints. Pick-up a shell casing, take a step. He reset an alarm. Don't step in blood. He was a robot. Waves of shock ran over him as he headed to the counting room in the vault. He was sweating heavily now. His ears were ringing. He was outside of his body, watching himself. He needed to gain entrance to an office, but he couldn't kick or shoot the door open. He kicked a hole in the drywall. This was not in the plan. At some point, a decision was made that he wasn't going to kill anyone else. He was going to take whatever he could get from the vault tellers, not touch anything, and get out of the United Bank Building of Denver, alive if possible before 10 am. His breath was short, and his voice husky as he ordered a man to fill a bag with money. He caught the #3 elevator to the 7th-floor parking garage. Then he disappeared into the morning of Father's Day, 1991.

FRIGID

A VERY COLD CASE

The 1991 United Bank Robbery
By Kimberli Roessing-Anderson

PART I

Crime

1

F ather's Day on Willow Street
        Father's Day (1991) would be the first Father's
        Day that I would not see my own dad. I had moved
to Denver, Colorado, in the fall of 1990 from West Virginia. I
spoke to him on the phone. It wasn't the same as sharing a
very rare steak smothered in Heinz 57 Sauce with him at my
childhood home in Charleston, WV. My husband, Brian,
and I got dressed and headed to his parents' home south of
Denver to see his father for Father's Day. We would be
having BBQ chicken and potato salad at their house in the
afternoon. I had a small garden in their backyard because
Brian and I lived in an apartment in Denver. I would weed,
water, and tend to my garden for a few hours and try and
avoid the Garter snake that had taken up residence there.

When we arrived, my father-in-law, Mike, was not home.
He had gone into work for a few hours to catch up on a
project. He worked at the United Bank Building in downtown Denver. At their home, windows and doors were open
to let the fresh air inside, and the TV was on a baseball
game. The local news interrupted regular programming to

show a developing scene of panic at the United Bank Building in downtown Denver. Police cars, ambulances, and fire trucks were everywhere, and newscasters indicated that the huge bank building had been robbed. Residents of Denver referred to that building as the cash register building referring to its shape. It is part of the Denver skyline. I had been to Mike's office on the 47th floor. There had once been a Peregrine Falcon nesting in his window sill, and the local news had been inside to take some pictures of it.

I'm not too fond of heights, so I never got close to the window when I visited. Mike worked as an engineer for Shell Oil Corporation. He was working on the Rocky Mountain Arsenal project at the time. He was occasionally in the newspaper with a picture and a story. Despite the traffic and living a ways away, he liked working downtown in the cash register building. As we watched the story develop on TV, we wondered if he was okay. It was before people connected instantly on cell phones by voice or text. He arrived at the house while we were watching the coverage and he joined us in front of the television.

What we knew was that a middle-aged man with salt and pepper hair and a mustache had robbed the bank and killed four guards in the process. The initial description was a white man, about 40-50 years-old. He was about 5'11 to 6 feet tall and weighed between 185-200lbs. (AP, 1991) We even joked that the description sounded like my father-in-law with salt and pepper hair and a mustache. Eventually, we went on about our day of BBQ and playing Mexican Train Dominoes. It was a Sunday, and we all had to work the next day, so Brian and I were back home in Denver and in bed by 10:30 pm, which was our custom. Most nights, we would watch the local news at 10 pm, catch the monologue of

Johnny Carson and then go to bed. That Sunday night, we watched more coverage of the robbery (now called "The Father's Day Massacre") and fell asleep.

THIS IS me in 1991 tending that garden on S. Willow Street
Photo by J. Brian Anderson, 1991

2

M assacre

ON JUNE 16, 1991, the fifty-two story United Bank Building of Denver was robbed. Four bank security guards were shot to death, and six tellers were held at gunpoint. Approximately 200 thousand dollars were stolen. At 5:04 a.m., an alarm went off at the bank in the records tunnel. Either William McCullom Jr. or Phillip Mankoff (both guards) acknowledged the alarm from the monitor room. Still, there is no evidence that any guard was dispatched to check on the source of the alarm. No one investigated it. The alarm wasn't reset until the robbery was underway. At 9:14 a.m., a man identifying himself as one the bank's vice presidents, Bob Bardwell, had phoned the monitor room and asked for entry into the bank through a freight elevator at street level. The man called the bank's guard room, using a white security phone located on the street outside the building. Security guard, William McCullum Jr. was dispatched to the street level to escort him. The robber then forced the security guard (at gunpoint) to take the elevator (elevator #3 was the only elevator accessible to the lower floors on Father's Day) back down to the sub-basement level where various storage rooms and the incinerator were located. The bank had stopped using the incinerator because of pollution concerns. The room had become a storage room. The robber shot McCullom (Denver Post, 1991). He hit him over the head with a large object (thought to be a flashlight) and left him to die near a back wall in the incinerator room. His death was so graphic that the judge in the case limited what photos the jury could see of William McCullom Jr. in death. The robber dragged his body during the murder from one room to another, and the possibility that DNA may have been left on the slain guard's uniform is conceivable.

After taking McCullom's security pass and keys, the robber then made his way through various tunnels to the area where the guardroom or monitor room was located. Two stairwells led to the monitor room. Stairwell C was the closest. At 9:20 a.m., he triggered an alarm in Stairwell C. Todd Wilson (a security guard) was dispatched to check on that alarm. The robber entered the guard room with William McCullom's pass at 9:24 a.m. and forced the two guards (Phillip Mankoff and Scott McCarthy) to their knees in a small adjacent battery room where he killed them both. They appeared to be watching a movie, "The Trials of Rosie O'Neill" with their backs to the glass of the window in the monitor room. Todd Wilson was returning to the guard room at 9:33 a.m. and was shot dead as he approached. "He was ambushed," according to the defense attorney in the case, Scott Robinson. The food he was eating was still in his hand, security keys in his pocket when the police later found him. The shot that killed Wilson hit a keyboard first. Before the intruder left the guard room, he took ten of the eleven VHS cassette tapes and other evidence that placed him there, including shell casings. This would be important in the investigation because police were trained to pick up their shell casings. The robber either missed a tape of William McCullom Jr. patrolling from earlier in the morning or left there it on purpose. He took bank keys, a two-way radio, and pages from the bank log. He had fired eighteen shots. One shot hit a door to a supervisor's locked office (Buckley, 2019). The entrance door to the office was also kicked, leaving a footprint on the glass. He kicked a hole in the drywall by the office door. The killer was unable to get into the office. All four guards were dead. (Denver Post, 1991)

Guard William R. McCullom Jr. was shot in the head and back several times. He was the first guard murdered but the last found on a second sweep of the building. Phillip Mankoff and Scott McCarthy were killed execution-style although it appeared that McCarthy had resisted after Mankoff was shot. It was McCarthy's first day on the job, and he did not yet have a uniform. He was in civilian clothes. The fact that he resisted also leaves open the possibility that there could be DNA evidence on his clothing from the killer. Todd Wilson was returning to the guard room to ask for help finding the alarm location when he was shot and killed. Each guard was shot multiple times in the back of their heads, backs, and arms. It was a slaughter.

The killer went on to the vault and entered with McCullom's pass at 9:48 a.m. (Rocky Mountain News, 1991).

This leaves twenty-two minutes unaccounted for where the killer had time to clean-up after himself, take evidence, and try to gain entrance to the supervisor's office. There were six employees in the vault, and they were told to lie on the floor with their eyes closed. The robber was calm but firm and told them to *"close their eyes and get on the floor.* He instructed them, *"not to look at him!"* He pointed a large gun at them. The supervisor, David Barranco, was made to fill a black bag with cash from the work stations. The robber wanted twenties, fifties, and hundreds, strapped. Five of the tellers were then forced into a small room near the vault called the "mantrap." A sixth (Nina McGinty) was able to hide behind a trash can at her station and eventually call the police. The bag was not full, and the robber left two million dollars behind in an adjacent vault. He left at 9:56 a.m. (Denver Post, 1991).

At 10 a.m., a different group of tellers would have normally come to the vault to collect and count personal and business checks from Saturday's business receipts. This was a standard business procedure for Sunday morning, according to Bill Buckley (former prosecutor from the Denver District Attorney's office). The group would call security for an escort to the vault. The robber made sure he was out of the counting room before 10 a.m. Buckley believes that this fact strengthens the notion that the robber had to know the usual routine of the bank. The robber spent less than ten minutes in the vault and left four minutes before that counting crew was to arrive. He went out the way he came through the other mantrap using the stolen security pass. The robber is believed to have escaped from the 7th floor of the parking garage, where bank security guards were encouraged to park (Denver Post, 1991).

The robber left the tellers locked in the mantrap. The tellers waited about twenty minutes and then began yelling for help. No guard came. McGinty was still hiding under her desk and mentally unable to get up and help the trapped group. After finding a metal spoon in the door sill, teller, Kenetha Whisler managed to pop the lock and open the door with it (Gerash & Goodstein, 1997). The hysterical group forced their way past another door, through stairwells and passages, until they were outside in a lobby and able to notify other guards and the police what had happened. Meanwhile, the group of employees from the check department had been trying to call the guardroom for an escort to the vault and got no answer because all of the guards were dead.

The chaos began in earnest as police came at the bank building from every angle. There was confusion and frustration as law enforcement was unable to gain entrance to some levels, and other doors were wide open. They cleared all fifty-two floors of the building. Everyone in the building was evacuated. There had been about one hundred people working in the building that day (Denver Post, 1991). They found Nina McGinty, who was in shock and hysterical (Denver Post, 1991). The police eventually gained entrance to the guard room and found three of the four dead guards. The found McCullom's body in a second sweep of the building, which left them without an obvious suspect. Denver police and the FBI had a daunting task ahead of them.

Approximately 100 FBI and Denver Police officers began the search for a suspect. It took 18 days. They interviewed over 50 former bank employees (Denver Post, 1991). An outside bank audit from 1990 had warned the United Bank of Denver of the benign access of former guards and employees to the bank. The audit told of the access to restricted areas by former employees due to incomplete records and master key changes. The audit also indicated that there were not enough dual control procedures (Denver County, 1992). Many of the audit recommendations were not instituted because the bank considered the changes to be cost-prohibitive (Denver County, 1992).

 The forensics challenge was mounting. DNA evidence was reasonably new as a science, but blood was looked for in every potential spot. In 1991, blood typing and grouping were common. Fingerprints were dusted for, and hair and carpet fibers were collected. It was quickly discovered that ten of the security tapes and all of the bullet casings were gone. Log pages were missing along with keys, cards, and two-way radios. It would not be long before the investigators, both local and federal, would know that there was little usable forensic evidence. All tapes that would have depicted the robber/murderer were gone.

 What they did find was a 7up can (in the records room behind security) (Denver County, 1992). A Mountain Dew can was propping open the control room door (Denver County, 1992). In the file room, a coffee cup was discovered (behind the security vault) (Denver County, 1992). A cigarette butt was found in the tunnels leading to the guard room (Denver County, 1992). A green paper towel was found in the incinerator room (Denver County, 1992). A security document was found in the left front shirt pocket of the uniform of the guard, William McCullom Jr. (Denver County, 1992). There was a footprint on an office door glass near the guard room and a footprint in the area where Williams McCullom's body was found (Gerash & Goodstein, 1997). There were a few random fingerprints. There was a bullet lodged in a supervisor's office door, and the bullets recovered from the four deceased guards. Unfortunately, there was no way to know when most of this evidence was deposited. Only the footprint on the office door glass and bullets could be dated.

Much carnage was left behind; four families would be devastated to lose a loved one on Father's Day. Deceased were: Phillip Mankoff, 41, William McCullom, 33, Scott McCarthy, 21, and Todd Wilson, who was also 21-years-old. There were six vault employees forever traumatized by the robbery: David Barranco, Kenetha Whisler, Maria Christian, David Twist, Chong Choe, and Nina McGinty. Every guard, former guard, employee, and former employee of the bank would be scrutinized. The community would wonder if the killer would strike again. The police were on high alert. Crime investigators and the FBI went through the crime scene with a fine-toothed comb. The media was at every possible angle. The public waited.

WELLS FARGO (former United Bank Building)
Photos by Kimberli Roessing-Anderson

DIAGRAM OF ROBBERY
Courtesy, Denver County, 2019

3

D escriptions, Sketches, and Line-ups

IN THE WAKE of the robbery, the six eye-witnesses were left
to try and identify the robber. Each dealt with the task
differently. The witnesses I was able to connect with
described a scene of complete panic once they escaped the
mantrap. When they finally found some security guards, the
response began in earnest. The rattled vault tellers were
sequestered in a private area. Teller, Nina McGinty, was
hospitalized (according to newspaper accounts) after she
was found still hiding under her desk when the building
was being evacuated (Denver Post, 1991). She was unable to
offer much help. McGinty denied that she was hospitalized
in her court testimony.

Each teller would take away something different from
the experience. Each would remember something different
about the robber and what he looked like, wore, or what he

said. The overwhelming feeling was disbelief. The tellers were brought back into the bank at one point to be questioned. This was when they were told about the murdered bank guards. The tellers wanted to know if the robber had been caught and why they were being returned to the scene of the crime if it wasn't safe. They were moved again.

The process of finding the suspect began with descriptions from the bank counting room and vault employees. The descriptions varied, but all agreed that he wore a hat (maybe a fedora) with a yellow feather. He wore mirrored sunglasses of some type. He was placed at about five-foot-ten to six feet tall. He was 175lbs to 200lbs. They all agreed that he wore a sports jacket of some sort (maybe tweed) and black shoes. One teller thought he had on blue or gray pants. One employee thought he had on a colorful tie, and while this sounds like a good start, there was an abundance of disagreement on colors, styles, and details. A few of the employees thought he had a bandage on his left cheek, and others thought he had either a real or fake mustache. He was described as having salt and pepper hair and sideburns. Some thought he held the gun in his left hand, and some thought he was holding it in his right hand. It was a lot for an FBI sketch artist, George Noble, to sift through.

There was a lead about a man that was seen by four rental car agents in Stapleton Airport (later replaced by Denver International Airport) on the day of the robbery. A man matching the description of the suspect was trying to rent a car with cash between the hours of 10 a.m. and 2 p.m. The man was said to be bragging that he had thousands of dollars (Denver Post, 1991). All of the rental car agencies turned him away (Denver Post, 1992). This man was never located.

Without notifying the prosecutor in the case, on June 20th, the FBI decided to have five of the six the witnesses look through two guards' "yearbooks" of sorts to ascertain whether or not any of the guards stood out. One book contained past guards (blue), and one book included present guards (red). There were about fifty guard pictures in that book. The images of the women were removed. The witnesses were unable to pick out any one man who they were sure was the robber. They picked out several photos and said that they looked *"somewhat"* like the robber. There was no definitive identification of any of the former guards. Former prosecutor, Bill Buckley was furious about this action because having the witnesses look through the guard books tainted any future lineup that included former bank guards. (Buckley, 2019).

By July 3rd, the FBI and local authorities had come up with a six-man photo lineup that included a former guard named James King. King was under heavy scrutiny by the local police and the FBI. The tops of heads were cut off of all six of the men to simulate a hat being worn. King was the only man in the six-man photo lineup who was also in the guard book (meaning that the witnesses had seen him before). Defense attorneys were not permitted to be present at photo lineups. A live lineup was problematic because, since the robbery, James King had shaved off his mustache. He had worn a mustache for many years off and on, according to his sister, Myra King. He had shaved it off before going to have a new driver's license photo taken because he had also recently misplaced his driver's license.

David Twist was the only witness that could be located on July 3rd, and he identified James King as the robber (Denver Post, 1991). Arrest and search warrants were drawn-up based on that identification, and James King was taken into custody later that night after a three-hour search of his home (Rocky Mountain News, 1991). Four other witnesses then picked James King from that lineup on July 5th. Chong Choe was unable to identify anyone from the photo lineup. These identifications would later come under heavy scrutiny from defense attorneys who claimed that the only reason the witnesses had picked King out of the photo lineup was that they had already seen him in the guard book.

Initially, after the guard book viewing had failed to identify a suspect, the FBI built a sketch of the robber by working with each of the witnesses. A sketch was re-worked based on additions or retractions made as each employee was given a chance to view the sketch. On July 1st, the sketch was submitted to the FBI. Then the local authorities looked at former guards and employees to see if they thought anyone matched the sketch. Eventually, they decided that James King looked like the sketch, and they began to investigate him more closely.

However, there were issues with the identification process from the start. Nina McGinty was the only witness not shown the original pictures from the guard book on June 20th. She was shown the photo on June 26th after the media had begun to show pictures of potential suspects and former guards. Nina McGinty was extremely emotional and unable to offer much assistance.

Four days after the robbery, Maria Christian stated, "... clear complexion with no facial moles or scars." Kenetha Whisler insisted that she was never shown the pictures from the guard book on the 20th (Denver Post, 1992). She was contradicted by FBI testimony (Denver County, 1992). At the time of the trial, Kenetha still believed that the photo had been removed or was not contained in the guard book she was shown. She also contacted a psychic about the case who insisted a female employee was involved (Rocky Mountain News, 1992). Whisler claimed that the mustache looked so perfect that she thought it was fake. David Barranco later said that he recognized James King immediately from the guard book but didn't want to "get someone in trouble" (Barranco, 2019). However, he also said that he thought that the mustache was fake. Chong Choe was unable to identify anyone. None of the vault employees noticed the prominent moles on King's face. The prosecution had an artist "touch up" King's driver license photo to make it look like the sketch (Gerash & Goodstein, 1997).

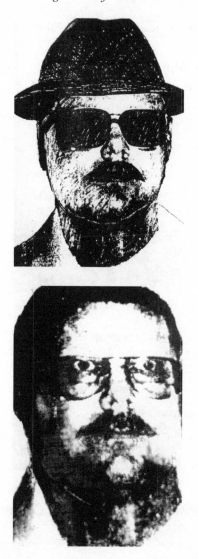

THE SKETCH by FBI
Courtesy, Denver County, 2019
A touched-up version of James King's Driver's

license photo touched up by DPD to look like the composite.

Courtesy, Denver County, 2019

James King from the Guard Book

Courtesy, Denver County, 2019

James King from the Guard Book

Courtesy, Denver County, 2019

THE SIX- PERSON PHOTO line-up

Courtesy, Denver County, 2019

Bucket of Ammo, Courtesy, Denver County, 2019

4

The Murder Victims

Courtesy, the Wilson Family, 2019

Todd A. Wilson was 21-years-old. He weighed about 200lbs and suffered from Nystagmus. It was his sixth day as a bank security guard. Wilson had worked in another department at the bank for nearly a year. Wilson had been employed by the bank the longest of any of the murdered guards. He was a close friend of Scott McCarthy and the best man at his wedding. The two often went to the mountains on their days off to four-wheel and fish. Todd Wilson was shot six times. He was survived by his parents, two brothers and a sister. When he was found, his lunch was still in one of his hands.

Todd's father had not wanted him to take the job at the United Bank of Denver (AP, 1991). John Wilson said that his son just told him, "Dad, I gotta make a couple of decisions in my life on my own." What made the murder most painful for the family was Todd Wilson's character. He refused to be slowed by his vision problems. He read books with enlarged print. The job at the bank helped him support his studies at Metro State (AP, 1991). Todd had just completed his second year in Metro's counseling training program and was passionate about the work, according to his father. Todd's father was unhappy with the bank's policy of using unarmed guards and hiring guards with little experience (AP, 1991). "I don't believe in guns myself," John Wilson said, "That's why I tried to talk Todd out of going to work."

Following the trial, the father of Todd Wilson (John Wilson) stated, "There is no doubt that police had the right guy." "It was devastating," he said. "I don't think they should ever give up until it's solved." When told of King's death in 2013, the elder Wilson said, "Good Riddance." (Denver Post, 2013).

. . .

In a high school photo
Courtesy, Ancestry.com

WILLIAM ROGERS McCULLOM JR. was 33-years-old. He had
been employed at the United Bank of Denver for five
months. This was a second job for McCullom. During the
day, he worked at Great West Life Insurance Company. He
was a computer operator. His family stated that he believed
he would move ahead by hard work and study. McCullom,
who was an A and B student, was working a second job to
pay off student debt. He usually would have left at 7 a.m.
from his shift, but he stayed late to help train Scott
McCarthy (AP, 1991). William Rogers McCullom Jr. was hit in
the head with a heavy object and shot multiple times.

McCullom was the last guard to be located after the robbery. He was the first suspect, and a warrant had already been served on his basement apartment in Aurora, Colorado, by the time he was located deceased in the incinerator room in the sub-level of the bank. Bill McCullom was single and had no children (AP, 1991).

McCullom's relatives described him as a workaholic. "He was an intelligent and honest and a very sweet person," according to his cousin, Rose Gay of Denver (AP, 1991). He graduated from George Washington High School and studied computer science at the Community College of Denver (AP, 1991). McCullom had also held positions at City-wide Bank of Denver and American Express (AP, 1991).

McCullom Jr.'s sister (Kim McCullom) stated following the trial, "It's as if the thing had gone back to day one when the bank was robbed, and the guys were killed. We don't know what to feel. The prosecution did all it could. There wasn't enough evidence, I guess." (Denver Post, 1992). More than 200 people turned out for his funeral at Pipkin Mortuary. He was the last guard to be memorialized (AP, 1991). According to friends, he had only worked at the bank for about five months and was unhappy about the guards being unarmed. Bill McCullom was only allowed to carry pepper spray according to a former guard (AP, 1991).

Even in death, McCullom was under scrutiny. The FBI interviewed his parents and his aunt at the Aunt's Montebello home. Bob Pence (who was FBI Chief of Operations in Colorado at the time) said that the FBI was not looking at the slain guards as suspects but trying to develop information and sequence. He noted that the same would be done with the other guards, but according to family members, that was not the case. According to McCullom's cousin, Rosie Gay, she was asked the same type of questions as the prior interview. The FBI wanted to know about McCullom's friends. She repeated, "He kept mostly to himself." (Daily Sentinel, 1991)

According to Gay, agents also went through McCollum's computer, business and marketing books, and his mail. Gay had removed the items from McCullom's apartment the prior week. Three agents interviewed the murdered guard's parents and aunt. They also went through all of McCullom's belongings. His Aurora basement apartment had already been searched before his body was located on the day of the robbery. It would be searched three times (Denver Post, 1991). The focus on McCullom was ironic as he was the only guard that passed the required licensing background check for the city of Denver (Rocky Mountain News, 1991). The other three guards had been hired in violation of the city's ordinance as no applications for them were found. In the weeks leading up to the robbery, McCullom had expressed worry about the security situation at the bank. "I hope I am out of there before something happens." Bill McCullom said to a friend shortly before the robbery. *I was unable to locate anyone from William McCullom's family to interview for this book.*

Courtesy, Ancestry, 2019

PHILLIP L. MANKOFF was 41 years-old. He was born November 23, 1949. Phillip was one of four children. He graduated from North High School in 1967. He was a father and a husband. Phillip was married to Susan Mankoff, and they had two sons (Ancestry, 2019). They divorced in 1985 (Ancestry, 2019). At the time of his death, he was married to Ann Mankoff and had a step-daughter (Denver County, 2019). He had been at the bank for less than a year. This was a second job for Mankoff. He took the job after changing careers and going through bankruptcy (Rocky Mountain News, 1991). During the day, he worked for Colorado Child Support Services as a section chief, according to the Rocky Mountain News.

From 1973 to 1990, Phillip was an Operations Manager for Colorado National Bank, Operations VP for Columbine National Bank, Operations VP for Interstate Corporation before becoming a children's advocate. Mankoff had been seen about 45 minutes before the robbery giving a new employee a tour of the vault (Scott McCarthy).

Phillip Mankoff was training McCarthy. He was shot execution-style while on his knees in a small room next to the guard room. His parents preceded him in death. He was laid to rest on June 17, 1991, at Emanuel at Fairmount. I was unable to reach any family members that had information for the book.

I can remember that my husband (who was employed by Manor Insurance at the time) worked for Phillip's first cousins and his uncle on the Mankoff side. Brian doesn't remember meeting Phillip personally but remembers the shock of the family and funeral service the day after the robbery.

Courtesy, Cody McCarthy, 2019

Scott McCarthy was 21-years-old. This was his first day on the job. He had been referred by Todd Wilson. They were close friends. McCarthy and Wilson would fish and four-wheel in the mountains on the weekends. McCarthy was married to Jennifer McElhaney, and Todd Wilson had been his best man at his wedding. Scott McCarthy wanted to become a police officer and hoped the job would help him accomplish this task. He didn't have a uniform yet and was in civilian clothes. He was shot alongside Mankoff execution-style on his knees. After Mankoff was shot, McCarthy attempted to fight back before he was killed.

Following the trial, his mother-in-law (Lauren McElhaney) of Littleton was angered. She stated that victims have no rights. "Why were the false ID cards not allowed at the trial? She stated that the prosecutors were limited in what they could show the jury. The system discriminates against victims. Defense attorneys can say whatever they want." (Denver Post, 1992).

PART II

James William King

5

T he Suspect
        Who was James King?
        One of the former bank guards was James
William King, also known as Jim King. His face became a
mainstay on Denver television for more than a year back in
1991-1992. Residents knew every angle of his face. His blue
eyes were studied for any sign of whether or not he could
have been the murderer of these four guards and the robber
of the United Bank Building. The frequency of his face
shown alongside the composite sketch of the killer almost
made them one. He was on the local morning news, the
evening news, and the 10 pm news. Sometimes, he was on
the national press too. His face was everywhere.

He was born James William Ette in San Francisco, California, in 1936 (Ancestry, 2019). Early on, he was the unfortu-
nate subject of his parent's divorce. King (who looks much
like his biological father, James Ette) and his brother (Tom)
then became part of a mixed-family when his mother
(Doris) remarried (Harold King), and they had a daughter
(Myra). Harold King adopted James and Tom in 1940, and

they took his name. King had two step-brothers (Walter and Warren) from his stepfather's first marriage. Warren died when he was a baby from crib death. Walter lived with his biological mother (Ancestry, 2019).

Looking through old family photos of James King, he seems like any boy growing up in the '40s and '50s. He had curly blonde hair as a young boy. He had big blue eyes. He smiled and looked happy. He is pictured holding the family's cats and dogs with his brother, Tom. His sister, Myra, was right alongside them, posing for the camera. Jim and Tom wore Hawaiian or striped shirts, and they whipped their hair into a Beach Boy type wave in the front. Myra wore 50's style dresses. In some pictures, the family pets are crawling around their necks. Their mother and father posed with them, and they appeared to be a happy family.

There were photos taken in Guam where Harold King was stationed in the military. There were photos in California and Colorado. The three children looked happy and as if they were growing up in any wholesome American household in the country. Looking at the photos reminded me of the black and white 50's TV shows. There were similar clothes, houses, and furnishings. None of those childhood pictures indicated that James King would grow-up to be a bank robber or murderer of four guards in his later life.

His sister, Myra, described him as mild-mannered. She said that Jim was a great brother. He was diplomatic. When the other kids got into arguments, he was able to settle things in a non-violent way," she said. Myra stated that when Jim was only ten-years-old, their mother allowed Jim to walk to the nursery school and pick her up and walk her home. Jim's mother thought Jim was very responsible. "Jim was trustworthy," She said. Myra said that Jim babysat her and Tom when their parents were out. "We knew who was in charge but not because he was mean about it."

"Jim started playing chess as a kid," Myra said. "He taught me to play when I was a kid, too," Myra said that she was never as good as Jim, and she could only move the chess pieces around the board. She said that Jim loved chess and referred to himself as a "nerd." He didn't play sports. He was more a bookworm and a chess player. Myra remembered that when Jim came home from the army, he had a big trunk full of trinkets and comic books. "He loved comic books." She said.

Speaking about his police career, Myra stated that Jim was logical and fair. He didn't like to use violence. "I was married to a macho-cop," Myra said, "Jim was not a macho-cop," Myra stated that Jim treated Carol like a queen. In turn, everything was about Jim with Carol. They had a very good marriage. Jim was so devastated by her death (from emphysema) in 2009; he was unable to attend the funeral. Already suffering from dementia, Jim didn't want to grieve in front of others. According to Myra, when Carol died, Jim called her and said, "They killed her." She had no idea what Jim meant. Jim would steadily decline after Carol's death.

Carol had been the first to notice Jim's dementia. She called Myra and said that Jim was having trouble keeping the checkbook. Jim had always taken care of all of the finances. Carol was not sure what to do. Eventually, a diagnosis would come that would confirm Carol's concerns. Carol was already sick with emphysema. The two took care of each other. However, after the trial, Jim didn't feel safe and discussed putting bars on the windows at their home. They also considered moving away from Colorado.

After the trial, James King didn't leave the house much. His neighbors and friends stood by him. Myra said that the neighbors knew it couldn't have been him. Jim still spoke to neighbors from his yard. He and Carol only went to two restaurants. They were places that treated Jim normally, and people didn't bother him or stare. Myra got a firsthand experience with the way people looked at her brother when they were driving in the car. She was in the backseat and watched a couple do a "doubletake" when they realized who was sitting in the car beside them. Jim wanted to move (following the trial), but Carol wouldn't do it. She wanted to be near family.

Myra remembered one episode when Jim was ill with dementia, and they were all visiting together with family. Out of nowhere, Jim stated, "They say I robbed a bank and killed people." "I never did that." The family assured Jim that they believed him and changed the subject before Jim became too upset. When James King passed away in 2013, there was a small group of friends and family that attended a graveside memorial. News of the death was kept quiet for as long as possible to prevent a circus with the media.

Jim had no relationship with his biological father. He wasn't interested. Jim had no memory of him. According to Myra, James Ette had been a violent man who beat his wife and two sons. This why Doris Ette left and took her sons with her. Harold King was Jim's father, according to Myra. The family bounced around a bit, and King transferred schools several times. After his high school graduation in 1954 from Castlemont High School in Oakland, CA, King joined the Army (Ancestry, 2019). He trained as a military policeman and was stationed as a security guard in Germany (Ancestry, 2019). King was honorably discharged in 1957 (Ancestry, 2019).

James Elmer Ette (Jim King's biological father) Doris
Ette and James as a toddler, Courtesy, Myra Church, 2019

Tom, Harold King, Myra, and Jim with pets
Courtesy, Myra Church, 2019

JAMES KING in the Army 1954-1957
Courtesy, Myra Church, 2019

AFTER THREE YEARS OF COLLEGE, King joined the Denver
Police Department in 1961 (Denver County, 1992). He graduated first in his class of cadets. Policing would be his career.
Aside from one incident early on where he fired his service
weapon in the air to scare a fleeing subject, King was never
in trouble with his superiors. That was also the only time he
fired his service weapon in the line of duty (Denver County,
1992). He would wear the uniform and police Denver in one
way or another for twenty-five years. He would work his way
up to Sergeant in 1975. He would try to make Lieutenant, but
while he passed the written exam, he failed the oral exercise
(Gerash & Goodstein, 1997). James King would stop a bank
robbery in 1973 while moonlighting for a different bank, and
he received commendations from the DPD and the FBI. He
was also the Sergeant of the ID Bureau, which became
important during the investigation because James King had

several fake IDs made with his picture but false names (Buckley, 2019). James King retired in 1986.

King would marry his wife, Carol Ann Guida, in 1962. They had three sons: James Williams Jr. in 1963, Gregory Scott in 1964, and David Edward in 1966 (Tom King, 2019). King and his family maintained what would be called a typical middle- class life while their boys were growing up. King had various part-time jobs during his police career to help supplement his income. He was a security guard for another bank, a radio announcer for traffic, and a security guard at a hospital (Denver County, 1992). Carol worked at Weight Watchers (Denver County, 1992). At the time of the trial, King had owned his 1978 Ford Fiesta for six years.

The Kings had some financial issues that ended in bankruptcy in the late- 1980's, and they moved to a slightly smaller home on Juniper Street in Golden, Colorado. By 1990, their three sons were grown, and only one (David) was still living at home. He seemed to be there by choice and not a necessity. King had worked as a draftsman for a map company (Maps Unlimited) after he retired from the DPD in 1986. He did that work for three years until he began having trouble with his eyesight (Gerash & Goodstein, 1997). It was at that point that King went to work for the United Bank of Denver as a security guard in 1989 (Denver County, 1992). He worked weekends from July 20, 1989, until August 12, 1990 (Denver County, 1991).

Even after filing bankruptcy in 1987, Jim and Carol still had debt. They still owed over ninety thousand dollars. Over sixty thousand dollars was for their home on Juniper. The rest (over thirty thousand dollars) was credit card type debt (Rocky Mountain News, 1991). The King family had about $3,500 in assets. With a Twenty-thousand-dollar pension and what Carol brought home from her job at

Weight Watchers, James King still worked part-time to make ends meet. Carol had worked at Weight Watchers for seven years.

James W. King as police officer early in his career
Courtesy, Myra Church, 2019

James King in later years
Courtesy, Myra King, 2019
The King Family, Greg, James Jr, Jim,
And Carol-clockwise, courtesy, Myra King, 2019
Last, James and Carol, courtesy Myra King, 2019

6

W hy James King?
Out of all of the guards, former guards, and other former employees, why James W. King? Setting aside the fact that the robbery could have been committed by a person with no connection to United Bank whatsoever, Jim King was a quiet, personable man. He had only worked at the United Bank of Denver for about a year (a year before the robbery) and had no issues with the bank when he resigned. He served his country in the Army. He never had any trouble in the military and was discharged honorably in 1957. He attended college and always seemed to have a job. King had no problem with the law. His neighbors liked him and viewed him as a responsible property owner who was friendly. He was a police officer in Denver for 25 years. He retired as a sergeant and had no disciplinary issues on record. Jim King may not have been the most popular officer on the force, but he had no complaints against him, and he never fired his service weapon at a person in the line of duty. There were no exces-

sive force complaints lodged against him. He retired with his full pension.

Nothing came out during the investigation or trial that indicated that Jim was a bad father or husband. According to Phil Goodstein, co-author of Murders in the Bank Vault, and other historical books about Denver, King was estranged from one of his sons, Gregory Scott King. This was his middle son, but there were even some questions about the estrangement being a misunderstanding because Jim King referred to his middle son, *as the one with tattoos.* Jim King said that he loved all of his sons. King's family was supportive during the trial. The bench behind James King, during his trial, was always full of family. According to Myra, the sons took turns coming to court because they all had jobs and needed to work. Aside from financial troubles in the late-80's, James King looked like a normal middle-aged father living in a middle-class neighborhood who liked to work in his yard with his wife. According to trial testimony, he liked to put together model trains. At one time, he had played chess at the Capitol Hill Community Center and belonged to the Denver Chess Club. King would say that he gave up across the board chess because he was working grave-yard shifts at the airport as a police officer. He gave up correspondence chess because he realized he was playing computers and not people.

One of the investigative techniques used by the FBI to try and find the robber of the United Bank Building was to take the sketch put together by the witnesses through a sketch artist and then compare it to pictures of the guard book. FBI and local authorities were already crawling all over former guards and employees of the bank. Still, at some point, investigators determined that James King looked like the sketch. This revelation brought heavier scrutiny. The FBI had already been to visit Jim King as had some reporters. Still, after the likeness to the sketch was realized, the investigation began for real. King was quoted in the Denver Post as being surprised how quickly the reporters had found him as he had an unlisted phone number.

After the FBI interviewed King, he shaved off his mustache. He had worn a mustache for years, on and off (Church, 2019). He would later state that he had been suffering from pimples and acne underneath the hair and had decided to shave it off for a while. At about the same time, King lost his driver's license, so when he went to have a new one made, he no longer had the facial hair. The mustache is a focal point of the sketch, and this sudden change in Jim King's look was suspicious to the police. This also made a live line-up almost impossible unless they were going to put a fake mustache on James King. According to Bill Buckley, this is the reason a photo line-up was used instead (Buckley, 2019).

James King purchased a .38 revolver around the time he joined the police force. He carried it for 25 years, only having to fire it at the practice range. As was the practice, he also carried two speed loaders, which amounted to eighteen rounds (Buckley, 2019). Buckley also emphasized the strong bond a police officer has with their service weapon and how many police officers keep their service weapon throughout their entire lives (Buckley, 2019). King had claimed that he had begun to have issues with the gun. He submitted his weapon for inspections, and in 1989, had a firing issue repaired (Gerash & Goodstein, 1997). King testified that he first noticed the cracked cylinder while he was cleaning his gun about a week after firing it at the range in June of 1990.

When police and the FBI asked James King for his service revolver, King stated that he had taken it apart and disposed of it because it had a cracked cylinder. Because this was the same type of weapon used in the murders of the four bank guards during the robbery, investigators were again suspicious. Jim's wife, Carol, believed it to be in a lockbox in the house. King claimed it was at Carol's urging that he got rid of it (Denver Post, 1992). Bill Buckley believed that a careful officer would have turned it in to the police department if the firearm was a danger and not thrown it in the trash. He also found it hard to believe that a police officer would dispose of his service revolver of 25 years in that manner (Buckley, 2019).

King would be asked during the trial what he did with the eighteen rounds of ammunition that he took when he retired. He explained that after he took apart and disposed of his weapon, he disposed of the ammo too. The prosecutor was incredulous that King would toss out eighteen rounds of live ammunition to the trash. King corrected him and stated that he emptied each round first and then threw it away. The prosecutor said that this was not believable. King's attorney argued that King was a conscientious man, and this was precisely the type of thing he would do. His attorney stated that King taped a fire extinguisher to the underside of the dashboard of his car.

Bill Buckley had described James King's police career as lackluster. He stated that King was a mediocre police officer and a mediocre sergeant. "For someone who bragged at cadet graduation that he was going to be "Police Chief," one day, he didn't accomplish much." Buckley imagined that King was frustrated with his police career after 25 years of service and upset over his financial situation. King had worked much of his police career at the Stapleton Airport. This was the "Island of Misfit Toys" for police officers. Bill Buckley found irony in the fact that King thought himself an expert enough to be writing a police procedure guide. King was found to be writing one at the time of the robbery.

More important, however, was that the ammunition that had been used to kill the four unarmed security guards was "mixed" ammunition. Denver Police used mixed ammunition. According to Bill Buckley, every six months or so, police tested new ammunition for .38 or .357 firearms. In case of an inspection, an officer would always have the latest ammunition in their gun. The leftover or mixed ammunition was kept in ammo buckets at home or the DPD firing range. At the time, four or five different manufacturers were trying to develop ammunition that could be slowed down. In other words, they didn't want a "Hot Round" that entered a suspect's body, exited, and then entered the body of another person causing collateral damage. They were trying to eliminate heat (Buckley, 2019). The guards were killed with this type of mixed ammunition. Buckley stated that only a police officer would have used mixed ammunition.

There were other factors, James King had just requested a larger bank box in the days before the robbery. The robber wore a bandage on his left cheek, and King had a mole (among several others) on his left cheek. King was known to wander around the bank's security level (at United Bank of Denver) when he worked there and study the system. According to Bill Buckley, King visited every nook and cranny. He stated that it was because he was writing a police procedure manual. King's familiarity with the bank made investigators zoom in on him (Denver County, 1991). The FBI stated that King had first told them that his youngest son went with him and his wife to the cemetery on the day of the robbery. The FBI also stated that King had claimed not to know any of his neighbors but "Red." They said that King was "resigned" when he was arrested on July 4, 1991.

Jim King looked like the sketch of the bank robber. He shaved off his mustache in the days after the robbery and got a new driver's license. King would say that it was because he had been at the bank several times to get documents for his sons from the bank box that he lost his driver's license. Every time he had to get his driver's license out of his wallet to get into his bank box, and he figured he dropped it at some point in the process. His .38 was gone. He upgraded his bank security box in the days after the robbery and made several trips to and from the bank box around that same time.

King's alibi was problematic because no one saw him at the former location (Capitol Hill Community Center) of the Denver Chess Club. Mixed ammunition was used to kill the guards. DPD used mixed ammunition, and Jim King was a Denver police officer for 25 years. He would have had access to the mixed ammunition. King had been a bank guard at the United Bank of Denver a year before the robbery. He knew the inner workings of the security system, which was called "The Maze." He was ultimately identified by five of the six vault tellers.

The slain guards: William Roger McCullom Jr., Scott McCarthy, Phillip Mankoff, and Todd Wilson. Courtesy, Denver County, 2019

The memorial to the guards with the bank building in the
background,
photo by J. Brian Anderson, 2019

7

Arrest

JAMES W. King was arrested on July 4, 1991, at 1 a.m. in front of all of his neighbors and his family after the neighborhood holiday fireworks show. The FBI and local law enforcement interviewed fifty potential suspects over eighteen days (Reuters, 1991). As a search warrant was executed for three hours at his home, King was handcuffed to porch furniture in his pajamas without his glasses. It was a strong show of law enforcement in both marked and unmarked cars. Investigators took shoes, a computer, manuscripts, clothes, a gym bag, and other boxes and bags of various items from home at 665 Juniper. James King's wife of 29 years stood by him in a nightgown on the porch. She shook from fear and the cold night. Eventually, she was allowed to retrieve and put on a robe. They found about $500 in small bills between King's wallet and nightstand. King stated that he was going to use that money for an already planned trip to Las Vegas (Denver County, 1991).

James King Mugshot
Courtesy DPD, 2019

James King was held without bond and under suicide watch. King would remain in jail from July 4, 1991, until June 17, 1992, when he was acquitted (Buckley, 2019). According to Scott Robinson, one of King's attorneys, said that he didn't have much contact with Jim King and never visited him in jail. He and King had a cordial and profes-sional relationship. Robinson handled the more technical aspects of the case while Walter Gerash handled Jim. As a team, they had to fight back hard against early negative media coverage. Gerash tried to get King out on bail but was unsuccessful (Robinson, 2019).

King's son, Jimmy, was quoted as saying, *"I think he was just caught in circumstances. He is a great guy. He doesn't even speed on the highway"*. Jimmy stated that his father was innocent. Neighbors were skeptical too. One neighbor, Joe

Trujillo, claimed that he had seen Jim King on Father's Day morning doing yard work (he later had to recant that alibi when King stated that he was downtown trying to locate his former chess club at the time of the robbery). Neighbors were unified in their opinion that James King was a nice man, a good neighbor and that they didn't believe he was the robber (Denver Post, 1991).

A considerable ordeal was made when authorities could not find Jim King's passport in his bank box. It was later found in his bedside table in the drawer. It had expired. According to Myra Church, this is one of the many things that was leaked to the media and blown out of proportion. "Jim didn't have a valid passport in 1991 to leave the country," she said. King had not been out of the country since he had been deployed to Germany during his military career. The robber had worn a size 9 1/2 men's shoe, and King wore a size 10 ½ to 11 size shoes (Denver Post, 1991). Gray slag balls were found at King's home that were consistent with the carpeting at the bank, but there was no way to say when those fibers were left at the King's home. He worked there for almost a year (Denver County, 1992)

People who knew James King as a neighbor, co-worker, or friend were stunned by the accusations. They remembered him as a kind, generous, responsible, and non-violent man going back decades (People, 1991). Jim's wife would not discuss the case, but she did say, *"He's a family man, a good father. Never raised his voice, doesn't drink or smoke. The only thing he has ever liked besides being a cop is playing chess or building model ships with his sons. They've got the wrong man."* (People, 1991).

King's middle son, Greg, stated that his father presided over a "Leave it to Beaver household. *"We're a lot like the Cleavers, very close,"* he says. Son, Jimmy, stated, *"He's our security, and I don't mean financially. We still tell him about our problems."* (People, 1991). Former police colleague, Charles Nidley, said that King was always quiet, easygoing, and friendly. Nidley was in King's cadet class and patrolled the streets with him for a few years. *"When you were with Jim, you almost never got into scrapes, no car chases."* (People, 1991). Jim's mother, Doris King (who was 75 years old at the time of the trial), said the following, *"He'd do anything to avoid an argument. He would rather be diplomatic. He was one of the most non-violent people you would ever want to meet. Almost too good to be true."* (People, 1991).

According to Myra, Jim's stay in jail was difficult. He was kept in isolation because he was a police officer, and there was a risk that he would be attacked in the general population. For the first few weeks, he didn't have his glasses, so he couldn't read or see well. His cell was freezing, and he was only allowed one blanket. Myra said that he was cold all of the time. She also stated that his food was often served cold. King lost a lot of weight between his arrest and trial. Myra wanted to bring him books to read, but that was not allowed. Books had to come straight from the store or publisher. So, she arranged with a local bookstore to send Jim books that she purchased for him. Others would have a more skeptical view of Jim King's weight loss and change in appearance. He didn't grow his mustache that winter, and he had lost about 28lbs when the trial started. He looked much less like the police sketch of the robber.

Myra also brought up a subject (during our interview) that isn't commonly discussed. How society treats the family of the suspect in comparison to the families of the victims? In some ways, the family of the suspect are also victims, according to Myra King. There is worry, sadness, and circumstances that are out of their control. They have the same hardships of getting time off from work to attend the trial, a place to stay, and transportation for out of town family. Myra said that the victim's family had an exclusive lounge to go and sit in with coffee and snacks. They had their own restroom. The victim's families had a place to get away from spectators and the media. Myra felt her family was on full display at all times.

The suspect's family had none of those conveniences and only found out halfway through the trial that they could remain in the courtroom during breaks if they wished to avoid the media. They still needed to eat and use the restroom. She said that running into the press or witnesses in the bathroom was very awkward. During the trial, there was a female phycologist (Dr. Kathy Morall) that was evaluating Jim King's behavior at the defense table. She would sit near the family and click her nails together over and over again. Myra felt she was doing this on purpose to try and get a reaction. During jury deliberations, the King family would sit on a bench outside the courtroom. The prosecution thought the bench was too close to the jury room. They didn't want the jurors to come out and see the King family, so the bench disappeared.

8

K ing's Neighborhood

JAMES KING HAD a lot of support from family, friends, co-workers, and neighbors. King had lived in the Golden neighborhood for about four years when the robbery happened. One neighbor, Spence "Red," Wood stated, "A lot of people around here call him dad or pops." "He is easy-going and keeps his place neat and in order," Wood asked King (who was a birdwatcher) if he enjoyed hunting. King said that he couldn't kill anything, even a bird if his life depended on it (Denver Post, 1992). Another neighbor, Pam Gay, stated, "I am glad he was acquitted. I don't think he did it." (after the verdict) (Denver Post, 1992)

Roberta Trujillo was another supportive neighbor. She and her husband, Joe, had lived in the neighborhood for eight years. She had remembered wishing Jim King a Happy

Father's Day on that Sunday, around 9 a.m. (Gerash & Good-stein, 1997). She had referred to him as "You Old Fart." She also called Carol and Jim - Ma and Pa or Pops (Gerash et & Goodstein, 1997). She and Carol had bonded over the fact that they had both had breast cancer (Gerash & Goodstein, 1997). Another neighbor, David Bell, testified that he saw King come home around 10:00–10:30 a.m. while he was mowing his lawn. He was less confident on the cross-exami-nation of the exact time (Gerash & Goodstein, 1997). Roberta testified about James and Carol King having two small dogs that sometimes tussled with her dog. She owned a pig and brought some laughter to the courtroom while discussing the pig in court. Roberta indicated that she was up and out in the yard a lot, letting out her pets and often saw the Kings in their yard doing yard work and wearing straw hats. She saw them around 9 a.m. on the morning of the robbery. Since the robbery, Roberta always wears a watch because of all of the investigators questioning her about time.

People who had worked with King described him as a calm and collected man who was diplomatic. One of his early police partners talked about Jim King's ability to de-escalate volatile situations. Co-workers who worked security with him said the same. He was low-key and pleasant to be around in the workplace. King was described as an introvert who worked quietly. The supervisor who trained him at the United Bank of Denver (James Prado) testified that he didn't believe King was the robber (Denver Post, 1992). King was not even on the list of the first fifteen suspects (Denver Post, 1991).

Friends, neighbors, and family welcomed
Jim King home after the trial in 1992.
Courtesy, Myra Church, 2019

PART III

THE TRIAL

9

C ourt TV
The Courtroom Television Network, or Court
TV for short, was launched on July 1, 1991, at 6:00
a.m. Eastern Time, and was available to three million
subscribers. Its original anchors were Fred Graham, Cynthia
McFadden, and Jack Ford (Wikipedia, 2019).

For those of us who followed trials, this was Christmas
come early. This was a gift to backseat lawyers everywhere.
There was a mix of legal shows and live courtroom drama.
By the time the OJ Simpson trial came along, Court TV was
being watched by everyone I knew. I would set the timer of
our VHS machine and tape the coverage and then watch it
when I got home from work. Anchors and guests were
generally attorneys. The channel covered many trials across
the country, and the James King trial was one of those trials
in 1992.

Court TV first aired on July 1, 1991, and ran until 2008
(Wikipedia, 2019). Shows such as "Opening Arguments" and
"In Session" were a mainstay for the channel. Aside from
the OJ Simpson Trial, The Menendez Brothers Trial in 1996

was probably the most-watched proceeding and the height of the channel's popularity. Pamela Smart became a household name, and people would hold their breath, waiting to see what outfit she wore to court each day in 1991. Some judges refused to have cameras in the courtroom. The judge in the OJ Simpson Trial threatened to remove the cameras several times in 1995. I remember waiting on the couch with my toddler and my newborn on "Verdict Watch" for the "Nanny" murder trial in 1997.

The channel made many legal careers for lawyers who would typically have been unknown on a national level. Figures such as Kato Kaelin were thrown into the public domain. Lawyers from famous trials would write books after their cases, as they had created a following. Robert Shapiro was one (the creator of Legal Zoom), Johnnie Cochran had a television show with Nancy Grace before he died of a brain tumor in 2005, F. Lee Bailey (who was already famous from the Sam Sheppard trial) would eventually be disbarred in 2001, and Robert Kardashian (who died of cancer in 2003) but whose family gave birth to reality television. Barry Scheck and Peter Neufeld, who would lead the legal community in DNA evidence and innocence projects benefited from their exposure on Court TV. Leslie Abramson (and the way she used to touch the defendants on the back, chest, and shoulders) became a household name. NBC's Law & Order was the number one television drama in 1992 (Wikipedia, 2019). Phrases such as "If it doesn't fit; you must acquit!" were memorialized. Viewers will remember the Menendez brothers wearing pastel-colored sweaters to court each day. The nation was watching Court TV.

Prosecutors also became famous. Marcia Clark and Christopher Darden benefited from their exposure to Court

TV. They both wrote books after the OJ Simpson trial. When Christopher Darden came to Denver to sign copies of his book, my sister (Stephanee) and I lined up at the famous Tattered Cover Book Store in Cherry Creek to meet him. We met him, and he signed our books. He read a chapter to the entire group. Court TV gave us the impression that we knew these attorneys because we were watching them every day on television. I still have that book. Christopher Darden eventually became a defense attorney. Marcia Clark writes crime drama. The Tattered Cover in Cherry Creek closed.

James King's trial was aired on Court TV in 1992 (Wikipedia, 2019). It wasn't one of the most famous trials, and only clips from the trial are available on YouTube today. At the time, I taped two things every day before I went to work. I taped "The Guiding Light" (my favorite soap opera) and the trial coverage for the United Bank robbery. My husband worked for Manor Insurance at the time. The company was owned by the Mankoff family. Their first cousin was one of the guards killed in the robbery. He had a close-up view of the grief of the family. Unfortunately, I taped over the previous day's coverage almost every day, so I don't have much of trial left on VHS tape. Fortunately, the Wilson family taped the coverage each day on a new tape, and they lent me their recordings. Steve Johnson was the local Denver reporter for Court TV during the James King trial.

I watched all the 14 tapes. There may have been a few gaps here and there, but I watched most of it. Court TV anchors spoke about Mike McKown, who was also a former guard, being the first suspect in the case. He and James King were partners at the bank and became good friends. As the prosecutors and defense attorneys questioned Jim King, the anchors discussed alternate suspects. There was a lot of time devoted to McKown and Paul Yocum. Paul Yocum was a former guard at the bank as well. He had been tried and acquitted in 1990 of a robbery of an automated teller at the United Bank of Denver. Both men testified at the James King's trial.

I should have titled this chapter for everything there is an answer because that is how James King's testimony went over. I once thought that he is either the unluckiest man in the world or he is guilty. There are a lot of coincidences. There are many questions, and then they are many answers. King wore suits to the court that were too big and hung on him. I was looking at 28-year-old VHS tapes, but he seemed to have a black suit and a tan suit. He may have also had a navy-blue sports jacket with khaki pants. He had a few ties-one tan and one black. He owned a white dress shirt. He did not have a mustache in court, and his hair was cropped in the military-style he was known for wearing. He had no sideburns and no salt and pepper hair. It was blondish-gray. He often had circles under his eyes. He looked tired and rarely smiled. He had lost weight while in jail, whether on purpose or not, and he looked sallow.

One of the most damning pieces of evidence against James King was the fact that he had thrown away his .38 Colt Trooper in the months leading up to the robbery. King testified that he had discovered that the cylinder was cracked, and thus the gun was dangerous to have around the house. He testified that the repairing of the cylinder was costly, and the gun was old and worn. He had paid just over $60 for it in 1961. The repair was going to cost around $200. King had a .22 in his nightstand, and a .12 gauge shotgun locked up in his home. He testified that since he wasn't planning to work security anymore, he dissembled the firearm and threw it away in several different trash bags on different days.

The prosecution went to town with this testimony. They brought in an expert, and I use that term loosely as he had never testified about this particular subject before. He testified about the attachment a police officer has to his or her service weapon. He didn't think a man that had spent 25 years on the force would throw their gun in the trash. King had also testified that he emptied the ammunition for that gun of its gun powder and threw the bullets away. King offered his son, David, his gun belt and speed loaders. David was a gun collector and had several firearms of his own. When David found out that the gun had been disposed of, he testified that he didn't want the belt or the speed loaders, and they got thrown away too.

It seems ridiculous. However, King was known to be a careful man. The defense brought out in court that while King had made repairs to his firearms in the past, it was only those that were recalled, meaning that King didn't have to pay for the repairs. King testified that he didn't want to spend the money. The defense brought in a gunsmith, Ike Starks, that estimated the cost of repairing a cracked cylinder of a colt trooper at around $200. He also mentioned that he had been hit by a piece of a cylinder that had exploded at some point prior. This was unsolicited testimony from a prosecution witness that was unexpected and not appreciated by the prosecution nor the judge.

King testified that he no special attachment to his firearm because he never fired it in the line of duty. King spent about eleven years of his twenty-five years as a dispatcher and two years as the sergeant of the ID Bureau. He only fired his weapon when he was required to qualify at the gun range. His wife made him a shadow box when he retired that contained badges, his hand-cuffs, several IDs, and commendations. The gun was not in there, and there was not a space for the weapon in the shadow box.

The day after the FBI interviewed James King, he shaved off his mustache. On its face, this seems like a foolish thing to do. No one but James King knows why he did it. He testified that he sometimes shaved off his mustache in the summer months when sweat and heat caused acne beneath the hair. Carol confirmed it. King's barber, Neilus Rome, testified that King sometimes shaved off his mustache in the summer months.

Rome testified that King came in about a week after the robbery for his usual flat-top haircut. King had been going to Rome for haircuts for 25 years. He said that sometimes King had a mustache and sometimes he did not. Rome stated that he had never shaved off King's mustache that King did that himself. "It was always neatly trimmed", Rome said about King's mustache. The mustache was a blondish gray. His hair was straight with no curl at the neck. He saw King every three to four weeks except one year where King went to someone else after he moved to Golden. King wasn't happy with that barber, so he came back to Rome even though it was a long drive. Rome indicated that he had never seen James King with long silver sideburns.

The prosecution contended that he shaved off his mustache to change his appearance after the robbery. They argued that the visit from the FBI spooked James King, and that is why is shaved off his mustache right after they visited him. The shaving off of King's mustache caused a whole host of problems with a live line-up. The defense was able to show his police shadow box that contained pictures of King with a mustache, and King without a mustache has proof that he sometimes shaved it off, but the damage was done.

In what some would call a tainted line-up, five of the six eye-witnesses picked James King out of a photo-line-up using an old driver's license photo and a live line-up was never performed. Based on these identifications, King was arrested. It would be brought out at trial that a live line-up was ready to go with three men having mustaches and three without. Still, the prosecution decided against it at the last minute.

James King had an alibi that was problematic. He testified that he decided after many years of only playing correspondence chess through the mail that he wanted to go back to playing across the board chess against other chess players. He had not played over the board chess for several years. He had previously played at Capitol Community Center and belonged to the Denver Chess Club. His Father's Day gift to himself on July 16, 1991, was to go back to the club and play chess. He placed himself downtown and not far from the United Bank Building.

The chess club had moved years prior, and he claimed not to know that fact. He went to the door where the club would be accessed, and it was locked. The combination lock was gone. When King couldn't find anyone, he testified that he got back in his car and drove home. No one saw King there. A couple of maintenance men were working that day, and they didn't see James King there. Still, they admitted on cross-examination that they were busy were their duties and could have missed him if he had only been there for a few minutes.

There was a lot of focus in the trial about whether King ate breakfast before he went to look for a chess game or after he went to look for a chess game on Father's Day, 1991. His wife placed him at home at 8:30 a.m. eating breakfast. She stated that he left for the chess club a little after 9 a.m. There were many questions about when he and his wife did yard work on that day. A parade of witnesses was called to testify about when and where they saw James King in his yard on the day of the robbery. Most would say that they saw him between 10 a.m. and 10:30 a.m. This narrative didn't fit well with the prosecution's claim that King robbed the bank and murdered four guards between 9 a.m. and 10 a.m. Neighbors recalled seeing King in his yard working with Carol, and they were both wearing the straw hats they wore when they worked in their yard. One witness placed him in his yard around 9 a.m., where she spoke to him as she drove by.

Later that day, the Kings testified that they went to visit Mt. Olivet Cemetery, where Carol's parents are buried. They also went to Dairy Queen to have ice cream. King stated that he dropped Carol off at home and went to the car wash. Their sons testified that each of them showed up at some point later in the day and grabbed some dinner for Father's Day. It wasn't a formal sit-down meal. The sons brought girlfriends. They showed up in shifts. King testified that it wasn't until later that evening when he turned on the news that he discovered that there had been a robbery at the United Bank of Denver.

Much was made of James King upgrading to a larger bank security box in the days after robbery and murders. This box was located at the First Bank of Westline. King's testimony implied that a lot was happening at once. One son, James Jr., needed his birth certificate from the box to obtain a passport for work travel. That seems to be the primary reason for going to the bank box. Another son, David, wanted to start keeping the titles of the cars he owned and repaired in the bank box, but the bank box was already full. A bank employee offered King an upgrade to a larger box for a promotional price, and King agreed. James Jr. has been teaching King about computers. He has built him a computer and told him that he should keep his floppy disks in the bank box too.

King made several trips to the bank box of the days after the robbery and murders. Carol was on at least one of these trips but stayed outside to smoke a cigarette. The prosecution argued that King was putting robbery money in the box and then taking money out of the box when he realized he was a suspect. They argued that he upgraded his box so that he would have room for the robbery money, which was in denominations of 20, 50, and 100s. They put on a witness that had seen King carrying a green accordion-type folder in and out of the bank.

James King was soft-spoken on the stand but firm in his answers. He kept it short-yes and no sir. He did not expand unless he was asked to expand, and he often stated that he didn't recall. Sometimes, he had his glasses on, and sometimes he took them off as he often did at the defense table. It would be hard to know what his prescription was because when he wore the glasses wasn't always consistent. He didn't fidget. His hands were in his lap most of the time. I remember Jim King being on the stand and stating clearly that *"he had not killed anyone, and he had not ever stolen from anyone."*. For me, it was a pivotal moment. Despite the strong circumstantial evidence and all of the coincidences, his testimony and those statements were convincing. I have watched that clip several times, and I still feel the same way when I watch it. Jim King was able to look at the jury and deny those accusations. When he was acquitted, I believed that his testimony was one of the main reasons why.

When the case was over, James King and his wife went back to Golden to their house on Juniper Street. His sister went back to Delta, Colorado. His mother went back to Arizona. His three sons went on with their lives. James Jr. continued to work with computers and technology. According to family members, he went on to work for IBM and other large computer companies. The youngest son, David, continued to work with cars. The media and witnesses stated that there could be up to seven or eight cars in the King driveway at any given time in different states of repair. I do not know how long he lived with his parents after the trial.

Middle son Greg was a tattoo artist. All three sons seemed to inherit from their fathers the ability to work with their hands. King spent a lot of time putting together model trains and boats from the photos I saw of his den. However, Greg would have his own trouble with the law in 1999. He had been attacked a couple of times by the ex of his girl-friend, Robert Morvillo. On the third occasion, March 27, 1999, Greg was attacked from behind and knocked to the ground. According to witnesses, he was kicked in the head and body. A man who was watching nearby tried to pull the ex-off of Greg. When Greg got up, he pulled a gun from his pants and shot the ex-three times. The wounded man died, and Greg was arrested for murder. He made bail and waited. On May 6, 1999, the case was dismissed. According to the police file from Adams County, Greg was defending himself. *I have made countless attempts to reach all three of the sons of James King to interview them for this book. I was unsuccessful.*

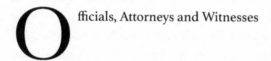

10

O fficials, Attorneys and Witnesses

IN 1992, the governor of Colorado was **Roy Romer.** The Denver mayor was **Wellington Webb.** The District Attorney was **Norm Early,** who was quoted as saying, "Crime Scene was the most grotesque horrendous I've ever seen since I've been in the city." The prosecutors on the case were: **Bill Buckley, Lamar Sims (briefly Craig Silverman),** and others. Ironically, I would realize during the research phase that Craig Silverman went to high school with William McCullom Jr. at George Washington High School in Denver. I asked Craig about this and whether or not this was why he stepped away from the case, and Bill Buckley took over. He said he didn't even realize that he and Bill McCullom went to high school together. Sims was a graduate of Harvard Law School. Sims hosted a jazz radio show and was a model according to Court TV. The police chief was **Ari Zavaras.** He had met James King when he was on the police force and described him as "quietly efficient" (Denver Post, 1991). The lead investigator was **Jon Priest.** He was permitted to sit at the prosecution table to assist and be a witness. He was called by the prosecution and the defense several times. He was known as "Speedy Priest" because he claimed to have driven from the bank to the King house in 12 ½ minutes. The distance was 11.4 miles. He stated he drove the 23 blocks, only hitting three of the twelve stoplights and did not drive much above the speed limit. He also had the nickname "Hollywood" because of his coiffed blonde hair he had when he was a patrolman. During the King trial, his hair was black. I tried to interview him for the book, but I was unsuccessful. **Walter Gerash** and **Scott Robinson** headed the defense team. This case and the coverage would elevate all of these attorneys to infamy. James King reached out to Walter Gerash before he was arrested because they had belonged to the same chess club years prior and had played against each other a few times. Gerash brought Robinson on board after King was arrested (Robinson, 2019).

Gerash was a well-known local attorney with a hot temper and brash attitude. He was from the Bronx and attended the University of Denver College of Law. He was a champion of civil rights. Gerash was a talented lawyer whose personality was bigger than life. His arms often flailed as he spoke, and I sometimes wondered if he would take off in flight and fly a few laps around the courtroom. He was cagey and on point. Gerash was ready to attack if there was an opening. He brought the drama and theatre. I got the feeling that the case became less about Jim King and more about Walter Gerash. Gerash treasured a good fight. He was a showman that could conduct all three rings of the circus with one hand.

After the King trial ended, Gerash stated that "Nine Days" was a record for a Denver District Court Jury Criminal Trial deliberation (Rocky Mountain News, 1992). He said, "He hopes King goes to work so he can pay me some of the debt he owes." Asked how much, "I'd rather not say, but it's in the six figures." Gerash declared (Denver Post, 1992). The King case would help make Walter Gerash a household name. According to Phil Goodstein, King and Gerash would eventually have a falling out when King wasn't able to pay him the $250 a month they had agreed upon after the trial. King's finances were tight, and during the trial, Gerash submitted a request for funding because King was insolvent (Denver County, 1991).

Gerash is in his 90's now and resides in assisted living. Still, some of his more famous quotes from the trial were, "Inoculating the jurors with a virus that is this so-called case." and "The media is part of an orchestra playing the district attorney's song." He was a media darling when he wanted to be, and when he didn't, he wasn't afraid to go after them. Watching Gerash on television, I would say that one word that describes him best is "unafraid."

On Court TV, he was often at a sidebar with the judge, making wild facial expressions and looking like what was left of his hair was on fire. He was passionate. Gerash was confident and not afraid to talk with the media when it suited him. Scott Robinson said that *Gerash had done a great job with this case (meaning the King case) and that they were "thrilled" with the outcome, especially because it was a death penalty case."* (Robinson, 2019)

Scott Robinson was the body of the work. Robinson was 42-years-of-age at the time of the trial.

Robinson graduated from the University of Denver and the University of Colorado Law School. He is a member of the Order of the Coif and Law Review. According to Myra (King's sister), she got the impression that Scott Robinson wasn't going to work on the King case. At the first meetings with the family at the law offices of Gerash, she stated that Robinson shut his door hard with his foot as the family walked past his office in the hallway. Myra wondered whether Robinson didn't believe her brother was innocent. She was pleased when Robinson came on board. Robinson would be credited with some of the most pivotal moments in the trial. When I spoke with him, he played that down and was quite humble about his participation.

Scott Robinson was the workhorse. He was young and energetic. Robinson provided the facts and the evidence to match what the prosecution was presenting. He was calmer and more rational to the jury. He guided witnesses and their testimony. Ironically, it was his showmanship that probably won the case for King. Robinson presented overlays of the disguise of the robber over the faces of celebrities, and some witnesses were unable to identify them. When I spoke to Robinson, he wouldn't take the credit and stated that it been someone else's idea (Dr. Edith Greene). Still, many thought that this experiment in court was what swayed the jury (Robinson, 2019).

According to Bill Buckley, Scott Robinson won the case for King. His cross-examinations were on point. He used overlays (with the bank disguise) on famous people to show some of the problems with eye witness identification. Some of the witnesses couldn't identify Harrison Ford. Others had trouble identifying George H. W. Bush, who was the President at the time Robinson stated that *"he was in charge of the technical side, and he felt he had done a reasonable job with that."* (Robinson, 2019).

Robinson said of King, "King is an innocent man. He's sensitive, intelligent, and he has a wry sense of humor. He doesn't have a violent bone in his body." (Denver Post, 1992) In 2013, he was quoted as saying, "My sneaking suspicion was (the killer) was a guard that came after King, and he had an accomplice." (Denver Post, 2013) I asked Scott Robinson about Paul Yocum, an early suspect in the robbery, and whether or not he felt that Yocum had committed the crime. "I don't know who did it, but presenting Paul Yocum as an alternate suspect was part of my job as King's attorney." He said. "Many thought there was as much evidence against Paul Yocum as there was against James King."

As I watched the trial, I noted that Scott Robinson was the calm voice in the room. He was the analytical one. He was respectful to the judge and to his colleagues. He was kind to witnesses from the prosecution and defense sides of the courtroom. He was courteous to the jury, always making sure he wasn't blocking their view of an exhibit. He could argue with the judge on a point or a motion for a long time and never lose his cool. Robinson could walk a witness through their testimony and then go in for the kill. He was well-dressed and had brown hair that was always neatly trimmed.

Judge Larry Bohning, Judge Brian Campbell, and **Judge Richard Spriggs** were all involved in the case, but Judge Spriggs oversaw the trial. Judge Campbell ruled that King would stand trial. Judge Bohning put in place a gag order as it related to photos, videos, and sketches of the suspect being released by the media before witnesses had an opportunity to see the line-up. He denied a verbal gag order (Denver Post, 1991). Judge Bohning also approved a motion for Jim King to wear civilian clothes in court (Denver Post, 1991). Judge Spriggs decided on the death penalty motion (Rocky Mountain News, 1991). When asked if he was glad the trial was over, Judge Spriggs said, "Am I ever!"

James Prado was a supervisor of James King and trained him (Denver Post, 1992). Jim Prado was a security supervisor at the United Bank of Denver. Prado also trained the four slain guards (Denver Post, 1992). Prado testified in court that he didn't believe that James King was the robber because changes had been made to the security system since King had resigned. King would not have known about the changes and would have most likely been locked in one of the mantraps (Denver Post, 1992). Prado thought that the killer had to be someone who knew about the security changes that happened after James King resigned.

In the wake of the robbery, the United Bank of Denver conducted an internal investigation. They fired a security supervisor. They dismissed two guards and suspended two guards (Gerash & Goodstein, 1997). The bank claimed that the supervisor had turned off a video recorder that would have captured guards eating in the guard room (which was not allowed). An anonymous employee made statements to the media, stating, "Quite frankly, I don't know how much longer I could have lasted there." "They wanted everything so squeaky tight so that they looked really good that they have forgotten the human part." (Rocky Mountain News, 1992). There was a tape gap found where guards admitted to eating in the guard room. The anonymous source gave the bank credit for security improvements and high pay for the guards. "But when you have guys who don't trust each other, then you have problems," the supervisor said.

The security hierarchy was as follows: **Alvin Lutz** (Head of Security), **Tom Tatalaski** (Security Section Manager), **Neil Tubbs** (Guard Coordinator),and **James Prado** (Training Supervisor), and the security guards. Most of the face time for the guards was with James Prado and Neil Tubbs. They did the training. Tom Tatalaski met with the guards monthly. Tatalaski answered to Alvin Lutz and carried out his instructions.

Maria Christian was one of the vault tellers on the morning of the robbery. Four days after the robbery, she told law enforcement that the robber had a clear complexion with no facial moles or scars (AP, 1992). She said, "No, I really didn't notice any moles." Christian also indicated that the bag carried by the robber was similar to a black doctor's bag. She did pick out James King's photo from the photo line-up on July 5. She did not pick him out of the guard book on June 20. I watched Maria Christian in court, and she was very expressive with her right hand. I could not see her face. She testified that she had been with the bank for two years. She had on a blue blouse and black pants. She stated that everything was normal that morning. She arrived at 7 a.m.

Maria was in the bank cage processing as usual, and she saw a shadow go by. She said that David Twist saw a man walk by, and he left the bank cage to go see who it was when the robber turned the corner and confronted them. Christian said that the robber was only three or four feet away from them. The room was well-lit with artificial lights. There were no windows. Maria testified that the robber wore a gangster-type black hat with a brim all the way around it. He had on sunglasses, and his hair was black and gray like salt and pepper. He had salt and pepper sideburns. The shirt was white, and his hair was collar length. He had a salt and pepper mustache. He was 5'9 or 5'10 and 185-190lbs. Christian testified that the robber wore a gray sports jacket, colorful tie, blue pants, and black shoes.

"I knew it was a robbery," she said. "I put my hands up!" Maria said that she focused on the gun. "He cocked the gun, and it clicked," she said. Christian said that it was a black revolver with a 4 to 5-inch barrel. She stated that she was scared. The robber went out and got the other tellers. "Who was the cashier?" The robber wanted to know, and Maria pointed to David Barranco. The robber instructed everyone to crawl into the mantrap. He wanted strapped money, no loose money, and no bait money. He didn't want ones or fives.

Christian testified that after the robber had the money, he brought Barranco to the mantrap. "What was he going to do with us?" Maria asked. The incident took about two minutes, she thought. The robber told them to close their eyes. Maria admitted she was peeking a little bit. She said that his voice was soft-spoken and monotone. She didn't think he had a deep voice but more of a tenor voice. His voice was threatening.

After the robber left, they waited a few minutes and then tried to escape. Maria tried the doorknob, and it came off in her hand. Kenetha jimmied the door with a spoon. Maria stated that the group fled up the fire escape stairs, ran across the parking garage, went to a guard station, and called police. Maria testified that she looked at the robber four to five times. Maria Christian then identified James King in court. She had watched the 9 News interview of Paul Yocum by Paula Woodward. Maria stated that it was not him. She thought Paul Yocum sounded clumsy and slow.

She said that Paul Yocum had a "fish mouth." On July 4, the FBI came to her house with the photo line-up. She first looked at #2 and #5. Then she covered the eyes of #2 and said that this could be the man who robbed us. The problem came on cross-examination when (like the others) Christian had not noticed any of James King 's many moles. She had stated that is complexion was clear, and she also estimated his height as much shorter than the other witnesses.

Just as I was closing the door on interviews, I heard back from Maria Christian. I spoke with her on Christmas Eve, 2019, over Facebook Messenger. She related to me that she thought the bag the robber was carrying was a suitcase type. Maria said that the robber had on a suit coat, hat, dark sunglasses. The robber was soft-spoken but threatening. Christian also stated that it had been so long that she couldn't remember the exact details. "I think King acted alone," she said. Maria is one of the few people involved in the case to feel that way.

Maria was confident in her identification of James King and is still certain. She was unhappy with the verdict, "I wasn't pleased with it." Maria took some time off from the United Bank of Denver after the robbery but remained employed there. Maria believed that King was going to harm them. "We just laid there and kept quiet," she said. She hopes the families of the guards can get some kind of closure, "because as bad as it was for us, it had to be 1000 times worse for them," Christian said. Maria Christian worked at the United Bank of Denver for ten years.

Nina McGinty was one of the vault tellers on the morning of the robbery. On a trip to the bathroom about 30 minutes before the robbery, she testified that she had seen Phillip Mankoff and Scott McCarthy touring the area of the vault. This was not normal because security guards usually did not come in the vault when vault tellers were working on Sundays. When she saw the robber, Nina stated that she hid under the counter of her desk. She was located at Station #9, where she counted food stamps. She was very emotional during her testimony. She sobbed and cried. She said that she went under the desk, knowing that she had to stay hidden. She felt that if she were spotted, she would be shot. She realized something was wrong when her co-worker stopped talking in mid-sentence (Denver County, 1992). As I watched her testify, even without seeing her face, I could see how nervous she was and how scared. She testified that a well-dressed man told David Twist to get down on his knees and belly. The robber said, "Stop Looking!" Nina tried to call to Chong softly, but she didn't hear her. Nina testified that she went under her counter and decided to stay hidden.

She testified that she got a very good look at the robber from the waist up on his left side. Chocolate brown hat with a beaded band and a yellow feather. She stated that he had salt and pepper sideburns, not fat but full cheeks, white shirt, dark glasses, diagonally striped tie- black and blue in color. She often referred to his hair as silver. He held the gun in his left hand. The barrel of the gun was black according to her testimony. She indicated that the barrel was twelve inches long. He wore a dark jacket. She likened his sunglasses to John Belushi glasses (a reference to the Blue's Brothers movie). Nina had to stop many times to gather herself. She cried and shook. She blew her nose and wiped her eyes with tissues. A box of tissues always sat at the witness box. She was wearing a light blue dress. She wrung her hands throughout her testimony. Her voice shook.

Nina stated that the robber was in his 40's or 50's. She thought he was about 6 foot 2 inches in height and didn't know the weight. He had a calm demeanor but authoritative. Nina said the robber said, "I want you to crawl on your bellies into the little room." He wanted strapped money. She didn't see a bandage. She thought she spent about an hour under the counter. She had to remain calm and in control. She eventually crawled out far enough to find a phone and call 911. Nina was shown the guard books on June 26 at FBI headquarters. Like the other vault tellers, she did not identify James King. She did identify King in from the July 5th photo line-up. Nina identified James King in court as well.

To the FBI sketch, she added the tie and the white shirt. She also saw the Paula Woodward interview with Paul Yocum and stated that he was not the robber. She said that he was not even close. Nina indicated in her testimony that she was not "hospitalized," but she did receive psychiatric counseling after the robbery. Nina testified that she could not return to the bank for questioning. It was too traumatic. She did not remember seeing any moles on the robber, and she was the only witness to indicate the robber held the gun in his left hand.

Nina testified that she could see King's moles from the stand. She also admitted that she had first stated that a photo of John Perpetua resembled the robber. I contacted Nina McGinty to interview her for this book. While she stated (on the phone) that she did work for the United Bank of Denver, she denied being a witness to the robbery. She said that she knew about the robbery, but she was not associated with it. Records from the bank indicated that there was only one Nina McGinty employed there.

Kenetha Whisler was a vault teller on the day of the

robbery. She is credited with finding a metal spoon on the doorsill in the mantrap. Kenetha used the spoon to free the group of trapped tellers. She claimed to have heard James King speak (at the defense table) and to have recognized his voice (Gerash & Goodstein, 1997). She wanted to testify as a voice or ear witness. She stated that she heard him say, "Where did that come from?" This was during the preliminary hearing. The defense was quick to say that no such statement was made by King (Gerash & Goodstein, 1997). The statements made by the robber were, "Get down on the floor. Who is the cashier? Don't look at me." The prosecution wanted James King to make those statements in open court. The defense would not allow it (Denver County, 1992).

Eye-witness faces could not be shown on Court TV. I could only see her from the chest down. She was soft-spoken and wearing a sweatshirt and black pants. Her painted nails danced back and forth as she moved her hands around. She identified James King in court. Whisler had seen Paul Yocum on TV and stated that he was not the robber. Her memory had to be refreshed a couple of times by being shown her FBI 302. She gave a detailed statement of what the robber looked like: thick mustache, black derby hat, sunglasses with black tape on the nose piece, dress jacket that was either dark blue or gray, black shoes, and black pants. She said there was a silver pin under the barrel of the gun.

Whisler remembered the robber saying, "Who is the cashier?" "Get the bag!" The robber wanted only 20's, 50's, and 100s. He demanded no lose money and no bait money. Whisler joined the others in the mantrap. Whisler testified that she crawled there on her hands and knees. The robber said, "Don't look at me!" She remembered that Nina McGinty and David Barranco were not in the mantrap when she got in there. After the robber left, they waited a few minutes and then started trying to escape. She testified that they ran down a hall, up a flight of stairs, through a fire escape, through a parking lot to the other side of the bank, and to the information booth. When asked to identify King, Whisler stated, "I don't have to tell you who it is; you know who it is."

A victim's advocate, Margorie Priestor, backed up Kenetha's claim of hearing James King. Priestor stated that she saw King's mouth move but didn't hear anything. For her to testify about King's voice, there would have to be an actual voice line-up. There is a legal process in place for voice line-up just as there is for visual or photo line-ups. For whatever reason, there was never a voice line-up conducted for the trial. It was not clear whether this was a prosecution or defense decision.

Whisler also insisted that she had never been shown King's photo in the guard yearbook on June 20 and that her identification of James King in the photo line-up on July 5 was unbiased because of that fact. She testified that she believed the photo had been removed. However, the FBI (Agent John Kirk) countered her testimony and stated that she was shown the guard book on June 20 (Denver County, 1992). Whisler also contacted a "cowboy psychic" named Jerry Ochs from Manitou Springs, who claimed that there was a female accomplice in the robbery who worked in security (Gerash & Goodstein, 1997). *I contacted Whisler, and she was not interested in being interviewed for the book.*

Carol Ann Guida King was Jim King's wife. She stood by her husband from the night of his arrest in 1991 until she died in 2009. She testified at trial. Carol stated that King had gotten up at 8:30 a.m. It was Father's Day, and he went to find his old chess club at the Capitol Hill Community Center (they had not met there since 1984) around 9:15 a.m. "He went there, and no one was there. "He waited for a few minutes and decided to come home." She said. Carol explained that they did some yard work and then went to the cemetery (Mt. Olivet) to visit the graves of her parents. Then, they returned home (Denver County, 1992).

Carol stated that Jim didn't own a suit or mirrored sunglasses. She couldn't remember the last time she saw him in a tie. She said, "He carried the gun when he worked at the bank. Then he locked it up in one of several strong boxes he kept in the house." Carol was in court, along with King's three sons, his mother, and his sister throughout the trial. One of the jurors I interviewed was impressed with King's family support system. When King was acquitted, Carol and King's sister wept.

To me, Carol King looked the most comfortable and relaxed of any witness at the King trial. She wore a white sweater and pants. She was calm and spoke clearly. She testified that when Jim went to play chess, he was usually gone about four hours. She stated that Jim came right back, so she knew that something was not right. She also testified that he was dressed the same as when he had left in s tee-short and shorts. He rejoined her in the yard to do some yard work. Carol testified about the trips to Mesa, Arizona, and Las Vegas that she and her husband took each year. They planned their trips with Action Travel on Union and 6th Ave. They would spend some time with Jim's mother and then stop in Las Vegas on the way back home to Colorado. The trip had been booked before the robbery.

Carol described how investigators dug up her front yard, back yard, and even at the cemetery where her parents were buried. She described the night of the arrest as difficult but also claimed to have little memory of it. She testified that her husband was home by 10 a.m. on the day of the robbery. Carol testified that they worked in the yard, went to the cemetery, and then to Dairy Queen to get some ice cream. She explained that on June 17, King got a larger bank deposit box to accommodate his computer floppy disks and David's car titles. She thought they had been to the bank twice in June of 1991.

When asked about Jim's mustache, she said that he sometimes shaved if off in the summer when sweat would cause sores underneath it. When challenged about why he had no acne in his mugshot, Carol testified that it had been over a week and that the sore had healed. She thought it had been eight or nine days after he shaved the mustache off that the picture was taken. She demonstrated with the police shadow box that he had IDs with a mustache and without a mustache. According to investigators, though, Carol told them in an interview that it was difficult for her to get used to Jim without a mustache.

Carol testified that the police and FBI had embarrassed her by showing up at her work to interview her. They showed up at her work on July 3, and they met at 12:30 p.m. in an upstairs office. She didn't understand why they came to her place of work. She talked about her son that lived at home, David. He worked at Econolube and also did auto work out of the house. On the day of the murders, David had gone to Supershots to get car parts. David used to work there. He left before 10 a.m. and told her he was leaving.

Asked if King had any hats, Carol stated that he a straw hat he wore in the yard and a police cap. She testified that she didn't know the last time she had seen him in a tie. She stated that he no tweed jacket and no mirrored sunglasses. They discussed King's shoes. She stated that he wore a 10 ½ and sometimes an 11-size shoe. Carol said that the police took several pairs of shoes from the house during their search. Some of the shoes belonged to her husband and some to her son, David. None of the shoes matched the prints at the scene, and the shoe size of the robber was a men's size 9 ½.

Carol also testified about her husband's health, stating that he had been diagnosed with high cholesterol in 1976. He was instructed by his doctor to walk three times a week. He even walked in the rain. She bought him a pedometer to keep track of his mileage. He was supposed to raise his heart rate above 140 for about twenty minutes a day, three days a week, if possible. He also had to give up regular Pepsi. He started drinking Diet Pepsi. She said that he had to start wearing prescription glasses in 1984.

David Twist was also a vault teller on the day of the robbery. He had worked at the bank since May 28, 1990. He was dressed in a dark blue or black suit, white shirt, and a thin dark tie. He was well-spoken. He testified that he went to Lakewood High School and had two years of college. He testified that the Saturday money comes in via the armored vehicle bank cage. Twist was familiar with the Markey card system. Maria Christian was with him in the cage. The robber had said, "No food coupons!"

Twist did not remember any moles or scars on his face. He testified that the robber wore a Bogart-style gray hat with a band and a bow on the band. Twist said that the robber wore: gray sports coat, white shirt, and tie, navy blue or black pants, and wore sunglasses. He stated that the robber's voice was calm and steady. "He took control," David said. The robber indicated that he didn't want any bait money. Twist testified that the robber used the word "mantrap". Twist remembered the most about the hat and the gun.

Dana Pappas was a former security guard at the United Bank of Denver. He was a prosecution witness brought in to testify against James King. He wore a white dress jacket and white shirt with a skinny dark tie and tan pants. Pappas indicated that King took notes at work. "Explored the bowels of the United Bank of Denver buildings and took notes during his explorations," he said. Pappas stated King would go places that he had no business being. King took Pappas to engineering areas. He saw King timing himself going from one part of the bank to another.

He played chess with King and lost. Pappas testified that King talked about robbing the bank hypothetically. This happened in the monitor room. Pappas testified that King stated he would call the monitor room, shoot the guard, go into cash-up (cash vault) and escape through an elevator. Pappas testified that King said, "All you have to do is call security." Pappas talked about the grip of King's gun. He stated that it was engraved with King's initials and last name. It read, " *J W King.*" It was pointed out numerous times in defense objections that Pappas had only worked at the bank for three months (from August-October 1990) and that he and King would have only worked together four times. King's last day was August 12, 1990.

Initially, Pappas told the FBI that he thought Paul Yocum was the robber because of the height of 6 foot 1, the robber being in his early 50's, and the salt and pepper hair. Pappas stated that he personally saw James King greet Bill McCullom on one occasion in the Monitor Room. The defense argued this is not possible because King's last day was August 12, 1990, and McCullom didn't start until September 11, 1990. Pappas had no explanation for that fact. I could tell that Pappas was getting angry on the stand as he began to rock back and forth. He had to have his memory refreshed several times by FBI reports.

Pappas also testified that he thought King knew Todd Wilson, but he backed away from that statement when he was challenged. He stated that King, McKown, Prado, and Yocum all carried guns at work. Pappas noted that King felt strongly that all of the guards should be armed. He would even pin news articles on the bulletin board when guards were killed in other robberies. The defense brought out that Pappas had been terminated for calling in sick too often. Pappas denied this and testified that he had quit. A memo stating that he had been fired was introduced by the defense. In my opinion, Pappas was not a credible witness.

David Barranco was the vault teller supervisor on the day of the robbery and murders. He was 25-years-old and had been at the bank for nine months. He had a B.A. in marketing from the University of Arizona. He was dressed in a black suit and tie in court. He was the prosecution's first witness. On Sunday, the armored tellers came to work at 7:30 a.m. The deliveries would begin at 8:30 a.m. The drivers would use the freight elevators. They would sound a buzzer and leave their bags in the mantrap. The tellers would then retrieve the money bags from the mantrap. They would verify the deposits. The process took about five to six hours to complete.

Barranco accidentally poured water on himself while he was on the stand and was furiously trying to wipe it off of his leg. He looked nervous. He explained that Nina was counting food stamps, and everyone else was processing checks. Twist first noticed the robber and asked Barranco if he saw the man. Barranco said he didn't see the robber just saw a flash of light and wondered if it was a guard. The robber came upon them and ordered everyone into the mantrap except Barranco. He had Barranco fill the bag. David testified that when he realized Nina was hiding under her desk, it startled him, and he felt as though he was going too slow. When the robber was done, he walked Barranco to the mantrap.

Barranco thought the black bag was 18x12. He thought the robber was 6 feet to six 6'1 with a gray or black hat. Barranco testified that the robber had sideburns and a military cut that was salt and pepper. He also had a mustache. Barranco thought the mustache had been glued on or that the robber was sweating. Barranco wasn't sure if the mustache was real or fake. He said that the robber had a stern, deep voice and a small adhesive on his left cheek. He thought the robber had mirrored sunglasses and a tweed hat with a dark rim. The jacket was plaid with dark colors. The pants were dark. The shoes were black with big rubber soles. Barranco thought the clothes on the robber were loose. The gun was a black revolver, and the robber cocked it as soon as he came into the room. The barrel was 6-8 inches. The robber pointed the gun at the middle of his body, according to Barranco.

When Barranco was shown the guard book on the 20th, he stopped on King's picture #16 and stated that the face was fuller. He also stopped on John Perpetua (a former guard) and said that he looked similar. He met with the FBI artist and helped create a composite. It took about four to five hours to complete. He picked James King #2 out of the photo line-up on July 5. Barranco then identified James King in Court. There was no response from King. His mouth was set in a thin line. Barranco had also picked a .38 Colt Trooper out of a four-gun selection shown to him by the FBI after the robbery.

One of the things that happened on cross-examination is that Barranco stated that he had a gut feeling about James King on June 20 but didn't say anything. He testified that he didn't know what held him back. He stated that he didn't want to cause a false arrest. Scott Robinson made Barranco admit that this was the first time he had ever said anything about a gut feeling. This was probably the only time during the trial that Robinson was visibly angry.

Robinson used a disguise over-lay on top of a photo of Harrison Ford to impeach Barranco. Even though Harrison Ford was a famous star in 1992, Barranco couldn't say who it was and looked shaken when Robinson pulled the disguise off. He also did this with George H.W. Bush, but Barranco recognized him (he was the President at the time) and Robinson stopped with the overlays. Because the prosecution wasn't made aware of this exercise beforehand, the judge was angry, and the prosecution was furious. The defense was told that all exhibits must be shared with the prosecution before they introduced them in front of the jury. The judge stated that there better not be any more surprises, but the damage was done.

Chong Choe was a vault teller on the day of the robbery. I watched her testimony as well on VHS tape. Although there was a language barrier, her testimony was relevant because she was the only eye-witness not to identify James King in the photo line-up on July 5. Choe was wearing a blue and white outfit and had a white and pink purse in her lap. She was very nervous. Her answers were short. She saw the gun. She said that it was black and had a 6-inch barrel. She testified that he wore black trousers, a black jacket, and black hardware shoes. Choe thought he was wearing gloves. She stated that he had a mustache and an English-type hat.

"I was the last person to lay down and close my

eyes," she said. The robber said, "Don't look at me!" "That's all I saw," Choe said. She testified that he had a soft, calm voice. Choe thought it was a joke at first, and then he put them in the mantrap. Choe said that the robber asked for the manager. Choe stated that the group waited an hour before they tried to get out of the mantrap. She thought the robber was about 5'8. She also noticed a band around his hat. She was unable to make an identification.

On cross-examination, Robinson joked with her that her English was better than his Korean. He tried to put her at ease. Choe stated that the arm of the parking garage was in the "up" position when she came to work that day, which was unusual. Choe noted that the robber had a clear complexion with no moles or scares. He was over 30 years of age. She didn't remember a tie. On redirect, Sims got Choe to admit that she has a problem estimating American ages and height. She said he was about as tall as David Barranco, who is six feet tall. *I was not able to locate Chong Choe when I was writing this book.*

James King Jr. testified at the trial. He was 29-years-old at the time. He was a Senior Instrument Installation Specialist at Air Sciences. He had been at the company for five years. He had graduated from John F. Kennedy High School and had gone to college for one semester. Most of his training had been on the job. He was a computer expert. He had given his dad a computer with a word processing program for his book-writing in 1989. James Jr. testified that he had encouraged his dad to keep his floppy disks off-site and not in the same place he kept his computer. They discussed putting his floppy disks in his bank security box.

He also testified that he needed to get his birth certificate so that he could obtain a passport for a work trip to Mexico. The birth certificates were kept in the bank box.

This was all discussed in June during various visits. James Jr. was single and did not live at home. When James King Sr. upgraded to a larger bank box, there was a key for him, James Jr., and David for his car titles. On Father's Day, James Jr. remembered checking to see what David was doing while he was there. Greg and his girlfriend, Rebecca, were leaving as he was getting there. King Jr. testified that his mom fixed him dinner, and then he and his parents watched Star Trek. James King Jr. did not end up getting a passport until January of 1992.

Danell Taylor, an operations manager, who had worked at the bank for twelve years, happened to come in on the morning of the robbery. She worked for Alvin Lutz and Tom Tatalaski. Danell needed to make some copies. She came in at 10:12 a.m. She buzzed the guards and got no answer. She looked for them in the cafeteria. She used a red emergency button that connects directly to the monitor room but got no response. Danell called Tom Tatalanski to tell him that no guards were in the monitor room. Around the same time, the police and fire department began showing up in response to the vault tellers escaping from the mantrap. Danell would spend the better part of the day assisting them.

She helped the police locate a crowbar and make access to the monitor room. She heard a police officer yell, "They are dead!" She was there at 5:30 p.m. when William McCullom was found. She finally left at about 8:30 p.m. that night. She explained that the machine that encodes checks is deafening, and that is why those workers didn't hear gunshots. She stated that she would wear headphones in that room because of the noise. Danell also testified that guards parked on the 7th floor as a rule. She said that markey cards were programmed for a person's job title.

When asked, she testified that maintenance, janitorial, and contractors also had keys to the building.

Roger Gottschalk was a security guard at the United Bank of Denver on Father's Day in 1991. He was supposed to work on Father's Day, but he called out. Gottschalk stated that he was "Stuck in Kansas" and would not be able to come to work. At the trial, he seemed quite cavalier about the whole incident until confronted with the fact that a man died in his place. He testified that King had back problems, and that is why he walked so much. Gottschalk testified that King sometimes volunteered to walk his tours for him. He stated that he also knew of King's health problems and that he wore a pedometer. He noted that King had made his own keys at the bank and that King had a curiosity that other guards did not have.

Bob Hoffman was a security guard at the United Bank of Denver at the time of the robbery. He was also a police officer. He testified that he and King talked shop. Hoffman stated that there was a lot of downtime on the job, and everyone talked about how they would rob the bank. He testified that King spoke about killing the guards. Hoffman did not fall under the same scrutiny as James King.

11

Three Weeks
The Trial
The beginning of the trial looked much like two tables of "Jack in the Boxes" popping up and down with objections, a frustrated judge, and a jury whose heads were moving back and forth as if they were watching a tennis match. The gallery was loud. There was coughing almost every day. It was the kind of coughing that makes polite people get up and leave in most cases. Horns honked constantly. A clocked chimed every 30 minutes. One could hear the rustle of people changing positions in their seats. Noise from the halls sometimes caused a bailiff to step outside and quiet people. When too many people were going in and out of the courtroom, the judge ordered the bailiff to hold them outside until about 10 people were lined up. One day a truck was beeping as one does when it is backing up. This continued for about five minutes. I could tell the Judge was about to come unglued. Finally, he sent the bailiff outside to say to the truck driver to stop the beeping and go away.

Spectators lined up to sit in on the trial each morning. A lottery system was used, and sometimes people didn't get in no matter how early they got in line. The judge would send the jury to the jury room when he was mad and then rip the attorneys. Then the judge would bring the jury back with a smile on his face. Once in a while, the judge would blow-up in front of the jury. Those were tense moments. Just watching on VHS tape made me uncomfortable.

Sirens of police cars, ambulances, and fire trucks sometimes stopped testimony. A phone would ring from an office behind the courtroom. Walter Gerash was loud. Bill Buckley was loud. At times witnesses were hard to hear. The judge was continually asking them to speak into the microphone. The judge would complain about the acoustics of the courtroom and make it clear to everyone that this was not his regular courtroom. Once in a blue moon, the gallery would chuckle at something the judge said. He was trying to move things along at a faster pace than the sludge in front of them all allowed. One could feel it.

Most people dressed up for trial. Almost all of the witnesses dressed up. I remember one guy wearing a white shirt and jeans. Faces of the eye-witnesses were not shown. The jury was not shown. One time, Court TV did show a few of the jurors as they were leaving the courtroom. Someone forgot to swing the camera away. I think it was the day of the bank tour. Also, during a hearing outside the presence of the jury, three of the juror's names were spoken before Court TV cutaway. Court TV was new and still getting it together, I guess.

Jim King looked passive, although he was facing nine charges for murdering the four guards and for aggravated robbery felony murder (Denver County, 1992). The six counts of menacing the six vault tellers had been dropped

(Denver County, 1992). His family looked nervous, and they tended to sit on the edge of their seats while others in the gallery sat back and relaxed. His attorneys had won a motion that allowed him to wear street clothes in court. His hands often wandered to his face to fiddle with his hair or mouth. In 1992, journalists still wrote on legal pads, videoed, held audio recorders, and cameras clicked. It was the era before smartphones, iPads, Apple Watches, Google Glass, and other technology that makes writing notes a thing of the past. If a journalist did have a cell phone, it was the size of a brick, and they would not dare have it in the courtroom.

The woodwork in Courtroom was a beautiful shining symbol of our justice system. Polished and regal, it stood in contrast to the reason everyone was there in court. The ugliness of the crime was an offense to the elegance of the room. As with most trials, for the victim's family, the trial is a place to be angry and grieve all over again. It is that awkward place where one sits within feet of the person who is accused of causing so much pain. It is a place where the victim's family can look at the accused if they can stomach it or if they dare. Usually, the families and sets of friends take up court behind either the prosecution or the defense in a show of support and strength. They are two teams pitted against each other in a battle that never really ends.

The trial began on May 20, 1992. It was the job of Bill Buckley and Lamar Sims

(as prosecutors) to convince the jury that James King robbed the United Bank Building and murdered four guards on June 16, 1991. Walter Gerash and Scott Robinson stood for the defense.

The defense was able to show that the prosecution had no direct evidence. There was no forensic evidence and no matching DNA. There were no handprints or footprints that matched King. No shoes to match the shoe print. No ballistics evidence could be matched to a firearm. Nothing from the robbery in terms of money or the disguise has ever been found. No relevant videotape evidence was left behind. There was no direct evidence.

The prosecution was able to put one witness after another on the stand to point at James King and state that he was the man who robbed the bank on June 16, 1991. Five of the six witnesses from the vault identified him. All five seemed quite confident that James King was the robber. When the defense crossed examined them, however, they were a little less sure. As the subject of Jim King's moles became an issue, the witnesses looked uncomfortable. King had several moles on his face, some quite prominent. Some of the witnesses could see them from the witness chair to the defendant's table.

The defense had James King approach the witnesses in some cases to get a better look. The jury also got a good look at the moles. A couple of witnesses looked apprehensive as King approached them, and the jury noticed that as well. The prosecution would argue that the disguise hid the moles or made them less prominent. One large mole on his forehead could have been partially covered by the hat the robber wore. The bandage covered another mole the robber wore on his face. The moles were quite visible in court, even on Court TV. They were prominent. He had five moles on his left cheek.

Gruesome crime scene photos were shown to the jury, and autopsies were explained in detail by experts for the state. Four Styrofoam heads were placed on a table in front of the jury. Long needle-like arrows protruding from the heads marked the entry of the bullets to each slain guard. Jurors look sad and uncomfortable. Some family members sat out this part of the testimony. Some family members sat on stoically on as some sacrifice for their loved ones. Jim King looked solemn. The defense had to let this testimony pass gracefully because there is no arguing that it happened just arguing about who did it. This kind of testimony is probably the hardest for the defense because they can see the jurors being affected and becoming upset. This is inevitable. Four men were gunned down, two of them were only 21-years-old. One of them was working his first day on the job. It was emotional.

The King's defense did not sit completely quiet. There were objections to testimony or exhibits they felt were too emotional for the jury and might prejudice them against King. They objected to statements and evidence that they thought was contrary to the law. Still, in the end, the jury was going to see the photos, hear about the autopsies, and see most of the exhibits. The families cried. Some jurors wept. This is probably the most challenging part of the trial for the defense to sit through.

Both the prosecution and the defense had a plethora of expert witnesses on every subject in the trial. One of the most convincing was an eye-witness testimony expert for the case. Edith Greene was able to explain to the jury how unreliable eye-witness testimony can be. The identification of James King had already been taken to task by the defense because the FBI had shown the six witnesses a guard book from United Bank four days after the robbery, which contained the photo of James King. Over the July 4th holiday, those same witnesses were shown a six-man photo line-up that included that same photo of James King. No other guards were pictured in the line-up. Five of the six tellers picked James King from the line-up.

James King testified, waiving his rights. For the most

part, answers were "Yes," "No," and "I don't remember." He was calm and professional during his testimony. King was polite. He explained that he threw the gun away because it was damaged (Denver County, 1992). He testified that he never killed anyone or robbed anyone. He testified for two hours. "He recounted that in the days following the robbery, he had told a reporter that he felt sorrow for the guards that were killed." (Denver Post, 1991). When King was acquitted, he nodded at the jury and mouthed, "Thank you." To the media, King said in a shaky voice, "I am relieved, and I want to thank the jury." King stated that he was tired and needed a long rest.

The Denver City and County Building
Photo by Kimberli Roessing-Anderson, 2019
(Where the trial was held and where I did my research)

KING WAS thankful for the jury and to "all those who have continued to believe in me." Jim and Carol could be seen looking jubilant, leaving the courthouse after the verdict. Neighbors welcomed them home with a sign in front of their house. King's mood turned angry later in the evening at his home when he told reporters, "I should have never been arrested and charged with the crimes. The justice system only worked because a jury found me innocent." He was shaking and visibly upset (Denver Post, 1992). This would be the one, and only time James King would talk to the press. He remained silent until he died in 2013.

12

5 3 Hours
  9 Days
  The Jury

Judge Richard Spriggs would preside over the trial. Over 200 people had been called for jury duty in this case. There needed to be a large jury pool, as this case was highly publicized and was a death penalty case. Voir dire began with a questionnaire. Having been called for jury duty myself, I can attest to the stress of just being called for jury duty. The site of the summons in the mailbox sinks the stomach. A juror has to advise their boss and submit paperwork to human resources, and there can be childcare concerns. Wages can be lost. There are transportation and parking issues. Once the right courtroom is found, potential jurors do a lot of waiting, filling out paperwork, and more waiting.

Having served on a jury, I can state that the stress only gets worse from there. Having someone's liberty in your hands is difficult. It is an awesome responsibility. It's cumbersome to sit in the jury box. I can remember finding it hard not to fall asleep, yawn, fart, sneeze, have my stomach growl, or to use the restroom. The juries I have served on have been two or three-day trials. Several times, I have not made it through Voire Dire. I showed up once about seven months pregnant with my second child, and the judge just looked at me and shook his head, no. I left. I can't imagine being on a trial that might last several weeks, being sequestered, or going through the process of being death qualified. However, it is my civic duty, so I have always tried to make it work.

The early 1990s was the era of the "Jury Consultant." Criminal lawyers and prosecutors were hiring them. These were people who believed that they could pick a perfect jury. They didn't even have to be lawyers. Some were psychologists. Some were journalists. Some were just lay people who had good intuition. Then cable news and Court TV started hiring them too. Mock juries became a thing. People were trying to predict which jurors would do what. Jim King's case was no different. Each side had a jury specialist helping them pick their jury. Walter Gerash was sending out questionnaires and hiring people to do phone surveys about James King. A lot of time and money directed to trying to get into the juror's heads.

After the death qualification in the King case, about 80 jurors remained. Each side had twelve peremptory challenges. The goal was to have twelve jurors and two alternates. The lawyers were given about two hours to trim that number down to the target. They ended up with seven men and five women plus the two alternates. Their backgrounds and ethnicities were diverse. They were death qualified. The judge was satisfied. The trial was ready to begin.

Of course, there was action outside of the presence of the jury selection. King's attorneys had asked Carol to find some photos of Jim throughout the years with and without a mustache. These photos were later stolen from a family member's car (Gerash & Goodstein, 1997). Myra Church found a poster of the suspect sketch hanging in the courthouse where potential jurors could buy sodas and snacks from machines. Myra told the attorneys, and the judge had the poster removed (Church, 2019). She also witnessed a prospective male juror walk over to where her brother was sitting behind the defense table and stuff his used napkin in King's coffee cup, looked at him, and walked away. He was subsequently dismissed as a potential juror when Church told the lawyers (Church, 2019).

There were a lot of moving parts behind the scenes regarding scheduling, motions by the prosecutors, and the defense. Would the jury be sequestered for the entire trial? Would they be sequestered only during deliberations? Would witnesses be sequestered? There were heated arguments between the prosecution and the defense, the defense and the judge, and the prosecution and the judge. There were motions by the media to try and get in the courtroom during the hearings and the trial. There were gag orders and leaks to the press on all sides. All parties were getting into position to play a game of trial by jury.

Being on the jury meant making sacrifices. The jurors were sequestered during deliberations. They had already been through a week of jury selection and endured a three-week-long trial. Their hotel rooms at the Warwick Hotel in downtown Denver had no televisions. There was one person in each room. Newspapers had to be scoured, and cut-up by a bailiff before the jurors could look through them. According to court records, the cost of the stay for the 14 jurors (including two alternates) and two bailiffs was $8,143.70 (Denver County, 1992). The bailiffs stayed on the same floor with the jurors. Jurors were not allowed in each other's rooms.

The jury room was located on the second level of the courthouse, along with the courtroom where the trial was presented. The jury room was quite dull. There was a conference table and chairs, two bathrooms, and a water fountain. "We didn't take many breaks." Jack Rushin (a juror on the case) stated. "We were there to do a job." The jury room had no soda machine or snack machine. There was no water except for the fountain and no coffee. "I used to bring a Diet Coke with me," Jack said. "No one was bringing us chocolate-chip cookies."

They had three meals a day out at restaurants and traveled on a private bus with the bailiffs. "They kept us isolated," according to Jack. Some of the restaurants they visited during that nine-day trial were: Liaison (in the Warwick Hotel), Janiquis Art Museum, Old Country, Mr. Smith's, Old One Fire House, Cherokee Bar & Grill, The Windows at the Radisson Hotel, Black Angus, Brittany Hill, and the Apple Tree Shanty. The bills ranged from $30 for breakfast to $300 for dinner (Denver County, 1992). The jury toured the United Bank of Denver during the trial.

After the trial, juror Steve Divide said, "I deeply regret that this difficult verdict will do nothing to relieve their grief and anguish." He felt compassion for the relatives of the four guards that were murdered (Denver Post, 1992). The jury forewoman (who has since passed away) stated, "None of us was 100% certain either way." "It was one of the most difficult things we have done in our lives." One juror held out for eight days. There were seven women and five men. There were 53 hours of deliberations. One woman held out for seven days. The jury- foreperson, said that if King is guilty, he will answer to a higher authority (People,1992).

Doubts that the jurors had wrestled with centered around the moles on James King's face. They had some serious questions about the fact that none of the witnesses remembered the suspect having the prominent moles. The jury was also influenced by the expert witness for the defense, Edith Greene, who testified about eye-witness identification. Greene spoke about stress being a factor in identification. She argued that the witnesses identified King because they had seen him in the guard "yearbook" and not because he was the robber. "The results of studies on the effect of violence arousal on memory are quite consistent." There is reduced accuracy," she argued. Greene testified for two hours and was paid $1500 for her testimony. This type of evidence had only been allowed in Colorado courtrooms for about a year before the King trial (Denver Post, 1992)

Greene testified that several stress factors could bias eye-witness identification. She testified regarding arousal, photo identification bias, disguise, and weapons focus. Her testimony was tedious at times, but she did make valid points about the studies she was presenting to the jury. One of her main points was that since the eye-witnesses had seen King in the guard book before the photo line-up, they were more likely to choose King's photo because they had seen him before. She also spent a lot of time on weapons focus.

Other concerns during deliberations were that some thought that two people were involved in the robbery and murders. Jurors wondered why there was no smell of smoke or gun powder on the robber after he had fired eighteen shots? A defense expert witness on firearms also raised these doubts. The jury temporarily suspended deliberations on the third day to review the possible bias of juror (Dorothy Stevenson) and whether or not she had made biased statements against James King to her co-workers before the trial (Denver Post, 1992). The judge subpoenaed five co-workers and spoke to Dorothy Stevenson in his chambers (Denver Post, 1992). Both sides wanted the trial and deliberations to continue. In the end, the judge was satisfied that she could be a fair juror. Gerash stated that if his client was acquitted, then everyone is happy. "If he is convicted, we will get it reversed." Gerash indicated that there were no funds for a second trial (Denver Post, 1992).

On Sunday, June 14th, the jury sent the judge a note indicating that the jury was stuck and needed a better definition of "reasonable doubt." Frustrated, the judge sent them a note back with the same definition he had given them during his instructions. The jury looked as though it might deadlock. There were indications that people were not getting along in the jury room (Denver Post, 1992). There were some tense moments, while jurors argued over the meaning of reasonable doubt. A few jurors felt as if they were being made to feel stupid, while others were acting superior in terms of knowledge. One male (who was a college graduate) was indicating that he was more intelligent than the other jurors.

The jury forewoman stated that only one vote was taken. It was at 10:a.m. on the 9th day after 53 hours of deliberation. The verdict was "Not Guilty" on all of the charges. The jury notified the bailiff, who informed the judge. The judge let the lawyers know, and they told the families. All started making their way to the courthouse as the verdict was to be announced around 1 p.m. that day. The jury had been out from June 6-June17, 1992 (Denver County, 1992).

13

C hess and the Airport
There was a time I thought I wanted to learn how to play chess. Sometimes, I still do, but if anything could turn someone away from chess, it would be the testimony in this case. Chess was made so complicated. Having so many witnesses come to the stand and try to explain the different types of chess, the different levels of chess, and the different chess club officers. Who cared? No one cared, and I am sure the jury was asleep, although watching Court TV, I could not see the jury. I believe the judge said, "eyes glazed over, " when he referred to the jury at one point during the chess testimony. It was terrible.

All that mattered was if someone saw James King at the one-time chess club at Capitol Hill on the morning of the murders. No one did. The prosecution tried and tried and tried to get witnesses to say that they had definitively seen King at a new location at 9th and Bannock in the years after the old location closed. One man, Larry Duke, testified that he thought he had, but he was just "guessing." He was a postal employee that appeared extremely unsure of himself on the stand. He chewed gum on the stand, and the judge made him spit it out. Duke made it clear that he wasn't sure, and Gerash got him to admit that he could have seen him on July 2, 1991, when Gerash and King played for the cameras at Ninth and Bannock after the robbery. Chess player after chess player marched to the stand and testified about chess. Some of the players didn't even know James King.

It is difficult to prove a negative. Without cameras on the prior entrance to the chess club, it is impossible to say that James King was not there. Even the groundskeeper testified that he was busy doing his work and could not be 100% certain that King didn't stop by for a few minutes. The jury was capable of weighing Jim King's alibi. It was a bad one. He put himself downtown at a place where no one saw him. The parade of chess witnesses was a bore. In my opinion, it made the prosecution case look weak because they spent so much time trying to prove that King knew the chess club had moved.

Something that Walter Gerash said to the judge out of the presence of the jury was interesting. Now, I am not a lawyer, but I thought that lawyers were not supposed to imply to the jury or the judge personal guarantees about the case. In other words, a prosecutor can't suggest to the jury that they "know" the defendant is guilty based on a fact that the jury doesn't know. It's like winking at the jury and giving them a symbol that you know something that they do not know. During all of this chess testimony, Gerash says to Judge Spriggs, I am telling you that he never knew about the 9th and Bannock location. I guarantee it.

The jury was not in the courtroom, but I watched that on Court TV, and I thought, how is that not the same thing.

Gerash was also a chess player. King knew Gerash from the Denver Chess Club. I believed that Gerash saying this to judge was odd. The judge didn't really react to it. Still, it seemed to me that this was Gerash giving some wink and nod to the judge and trying to influence his decision-making on the subject. The prosecution didn't react as strongly as I thought they would either, so I could be wrong. I thought it was odd. If Gerash knew it through his attorney/client privilege, then he shouldn't have talked about it. If he knew it as a witness, he would have to take the stand and testify.

The jurors I spoke to all agreed that the chess testimony was torture. Much like all of the time spent on ammunition, it wasn't necessary and made the trial longer than it had to be. The defense made a similar spectacle of the car rental debacle. They brought forth a bunch of employees from the airport and rental car agencies to testify that a man had been at the airport on the day of the murders that could have been the robber. He was dressed oddly and claimed to have thousands of dollars with him, but no credit card to rent a car. The witnesses described different heights, weights, and body sizes. They saw different types of clothes. The problem was that the descriptions of the witnesses varied wildly. This was a red herring too. None of them could say definitively that King was the man at the airport.

Judge Spriggs tried to move the case along, and he became especially testy during the chess testimony. The case wasn't about chess. The case was about murder and robbery. Chess was a red-herring. At most, it should have taken the prosecution one witness to establish that the club had moved years before and that if King received a chess club newsletter, he should have known that fact. The jurors

I spoke with resented the inordinate amount of time spent on three issues: ammunition, the airport mystery figure, most of all, the chess testimony. Watching on VHS tape, I completely agreed. I understood why the ammunition testimony was necessary. The chess testimony and the testimony about the man at the airport became ridiculous.

14

The Back & Forth

The Motions

The courtroom does not sit silent nor idle in the months leading up to a trial. Motions are filed by both the defense and the prosecution that shape the case ahead. Much of the work is done ahead of time and before the jury is selected. This trial was on its third judge before the jury was chosen. Some of the hardest battles are fought during this period. Gerash and Robinson lost quite a few of these early battles.

The defense asked for a gag order from the judge. Gerash was trying to control the leaks but also the importance that a sketch or picture of the defendant (James King) be banned from the newspaper and television until a line-up for the defendant had been completed. The prosecution also wanted the photo and sketch gag order. The media fought it. The judge approved the gag order for the sketch and photos. He denied the gag order that would have prohibited the prosecution and defense from speaking to the media.

Gerash won a motion to allow James King to wear civilian clothes in court, but he lost a bid to have the defendant released on bail. Jim King would spend a year in jail awaiting trial. Gerash also lost his fight to have interviews with King and law enforcement suppressed. Gerash argued that King has stated that he would like to have his lawyers present. He said that King's constitutional rights against self-incrimination had been violated. The judge disagreed. Because King had been a police officer for 25 years, the judge stated that the defendant knew his rights and spoke anyway.

Gerash lost the motion on the death penalty. He had argued that the death penalty was not the law when the crime was committed in Colorado. The death penalty had indeed been suspended, and the law re-written during that period. Still, the judge ruled that it had always been the intention of Colorado to have the death penalty for first-degree murder cases. This was a significant loss for Gerash. He then took the case to the Colorado Supreme Court, where he again lost. One of his big wins was the right to offer alternate suspects, and to limit the amount of information, the jury would hear about the two manuscripts King was working on at home before the robbery.

Gerash also had testimony from an old army buddy suppressed. The judge ruled that he wasn't going to allow words spoken 37 years before being used against the defendant. Another massive win for Gerash and the defense was the suppression of the six false IDs that King had made while he was the sergeant of the DPD ID Bureau. The fake IDs were found in King's safety deposit box at his bank. There was heated debate about the IDs, but in the end, the judge thought they had no apparent connection to the robbery and that they were too prejudicial.

These motions were not the only ones connected to the King case, and the judge's rulings on these motions did not mean that the arguing was over. The James King trial was filled with sidebars and arguments in the judge's chambers out of the presence of the jury. This was a feisty group of lawyers who were ready to battle at a moment's notice. They could argue the smallest point into the ground while the judge tried to push the trial along. As a spectator, I can remember the judge's face turning bright red at some points. He became frustrated with the defense and the prosecution in equal amounts.

It took almost a year to get the case from arrest to trial (this included a very contentious preliminary hearing). Jury selection would last over a week. The jury had to be death qualified. The trial had 16 days of testimony. This included a field trip to the bank. There were volatile arguments over the jury instructions. The jury was sequestered at the point of deliberations. These deliberations lasted nine days. Twice, the jury sent notes to the judge (Tuesday and Sunday) asking for a lay man's definition of "reasonable doubt," "burden of proof," and inquiring as to when a jury is considered "hung."

15

Alternative Suspects

The judge allowed the defense to offer alternative suspects as part of their case, and there were several to choose from. The most obvious was Paul Yocum. At the time of the trial, Paul Yocum was 52-years-old. When he testified, he wore what appeared to be a powder blue suit and tie. He wore a white shirt and huge glasses. His ears protruded from the sides of his head. He had thinning brown hair with a patch in the middle of his head. His alibi was that he was dubbing jazz audio tapes at the time of the robbery and murder in his apartment, alone. He lived downtown. On Sunday mornings, it was his routine to go to the 7 Eleven and get a newspaper.

Yocum explained that he rode the RTD and did not drive. He went to Skippers (a seafood and chowder restaurant) and a local bookstore before returning home at about 1:45 p.m. Although he had been tried and acquitted of robbing an automated teller machine at the United Bank of Denver in 1990, he said that he wasn't bitter. Yocum quit his job after the trial. Paul's diary told a different story. He was angry at Thomas Tatalanski, who was a security section manager at the United Bank of Denver, and Paul was upset that he was in debt to his father. Yocum stated that the debt had ruined their relationship. He owed his father thousands of dollars because of the cost of his defense attorney at trial.

Yocum testified that he didn't know any of the guards that were killed. When the FBI visited Yocum, in the wake of the 1991 robbery, they found he had a closet secured with a set of handcuffs. Inside the closet, they found: boxes of ammunition for a .38, a .357 type weapon, police batons, replica badges, surplus army ammunition, and dummy grenades. By the amount of ammunition Yocum had, the FBI determined that he was a re-loader and found his re-loading table in another room. Asked if any of his neighbors could vouch for his whereabouts Yocum said he didn't know his neighbors because they were transient types.

The FBI would visit Yocum three times. The third time, they had a warrant. Yocum was leaving his residence with a duffel bag when the FBI arrived the third time. Yocum told investigators that he had phoned his attorney and that his attorney had told him to fill his duffel bag with "some stuff" and leave. Besides what they had seen in Paul Yocum's closet, they found two diaries, five speed loaders that were loaded, two more Colt Trooper speed loaders, hollow-point ammunition, nine spent rounds, the loading table, scale to measure gun powder, 20-25 unfired bullets, and a metal box filled with ammunition.

Some of the quotes from Yocum's diary were disturbing. He referred to the United Bank of Denver as "Assholes, I will never recommend them as employers!" "Tom Tatalaski can rot in Hell!" Yocum wrote about hating the bank and that working there was like "Raking rocks with a 16 lb. hammer," according to an FBI agent that testified at the trial. Agent

Charles Evans testified that Yocum's apartment was a mess. The basement room was dirty and unorganized. There were guns and ammunition everywhere. Ammo, casings, and gun books littered the floor and shelves.

Paul Yocum's father had loaned him ten thousand dollars to pay for his defense, and he was trying to pay him back. When he received his back pay from the United Bank of Denver after his acquittal, he sent his father one thousand dollars of that money. Yocum said that he suffered nightmares about being convicted of a crime that "he didn't do". Yocum expected a large inheritance when his parents died, and he stated that he wouldn't need to rob anyone.

However, at the home of Paul Yocum's mother, more gun paraphernalia was found by investigators. Police and FBI searched her home in Flagler, Colorado, while Yocum was a suspect. There was more ammunition. Burned paper with the United of Bank of Denver logo was found in a fire pit at her home (Denver Post, 1991). They didn't find any direct evidence to connect Paul Yocum to the United Bank of Denver's robbery or murders.

Multiple neighbors saw Paul Yocum coming and going from his apartment all day. No one placed him at the United Bank of Denver. With Yocum, there were other items of interest. Witnesses thought they saw Yocum dressed in a dress jacket, pants, and black shoes on the day of the robbery (Denver County, 1992). A witness thought she saw a car similar to the one Yocum drove at the time (Denver County, 1992). Yocum's diaries were disturbing, and he did write some bad things about the bank and some of the employees that worked there.

No eye-witnesses identified him from either of the guard books or from what the court referred to as the "Paul Yocum line-up." Yocum was not arrested, and he is the one who first gave authorities the name of James King as a potential suspect. Yocum had health problems that may have stemmed from an accident he was involved in as a child. He was injured, and his three-year-old sister was killed in an airshow in Flagler, Colorado, in 1953. Yocum suffered brain damage and suffered from epilepsy as a result. He took several prescriptions for epilepsy and his heart, which the police noted during their searches. Paul Yocum died five months after the trial of a massive heart attack.

Dewey Baker, who was incarcerated in California for bank robbery, was another alternative suspect. Aided by his girlfriend, Linda Johnson, he wrote letters and made phone calls stating that he was responsible for the crime on Father's Day 1991 (Denver Post, 1992). Baker said, "I'm guilty of the crimes James King is charged with, and he is indeed an innocent man." He stated that James King was innocent and that he didn't admit it lightly (Denver Post, 1992). Baker noted that he was looking for peace of mind. According to his girlfriend, he had said that "something had gone wrong with a big job in Denver." Linda Johnson also said that he told her that "Four guards got dusted."

These admissions went on during the trial, and Judge Spriggs was not pleased. He didn't believe Baker and thought it was "jailhouse chatter." Spriggs told the lawyers that "We all have been around long enough to recognize this for what it is." Gerash argued for a mistrial. Baker had been in Denver at the time of the robbery. He was placed there by phone records. He also resembled the sketch of the robber. Baker had a mole of his left cheek. He traveled to San Francisco from Denver under an assumed name. Baker was also known to shave off his mustache after robberies in California. Dewey was being held in California on robbery charges in Federal Court. The FBI had already spoken to Baker and cleared him. The judge refused to order a mistrial (Denver Post, 1992). Baker eventually recanted his confession.

Harry Glass was a guard at the United Bank of Denver and an alternate suspect. Glass was 6 foot tall and about 150lbs. He was tall, skinny, and blonde at the trial. He wore glasses. He had a mustache and a mullet. He wore a white shirt and jeans. He was a part-time weekend guard. Glass had worked 12 p.m.-12 a.m. the day before the robbery and murders. He was supposed to work the morning of the robbery, but he was told to come in that afternoon instead because Scott McCarthy was training Scott McCarthy (Denver County, 1992). His fingerprint was found on a Mountain Dew can at the scene (Denver County, 1992).

When Glass was questioned by DPD and the FBI about the robbery, he became angry. He was friends with two of the slain guards. Glass ended up quitting because of the robbery, and what he thought was a less than secure system of security. He thought the guards at United Bank should have been armed (Denver County, 1992). "I guess I escaped the whole thing," a red-eyed Harry Glass told the media. "Three of my co-workers were dead; I never went back." Glass said that he knew the victims "very well." He did tell investigators about an incident that happened about a month before the robbery. He and another guard, Richard Rosenberg, filed a report about a strange man that had called the monitor room. The man asked about camera locations and codes to enter the building. The man had said that he was staying at the YMCA down the street. Glass said he never heard anything back.

On the morning of the robbery, Glass, who lived alone, had to take his sick cat to the vet. He testified that he took the cat to the vet and then went to King Soopers to pick up some snacks. When he arrived at the bank at 12:30, there was mayhem and police everywhere. He went to the 17th and Lincoln entrance. Police sent him to the atrium, where he sat until 6 p.m. He told police that he would drink Mt. Dew and then place the empty can in the trash under the counter in the monitor room. When asked in court- how many of his prints were on the Mt. Dew can, he answered, "I suppose all of them." Anticipating a brutal cross-examination, Bill Buckley asked Harry Glass if he had killed the four guards. Glass testified that he did not. Glass had been friends with Phillip Mankoff and Bill McCullom. Newspaper reports indicated that Glass had been out with Bill McCullom the night before the murders. Glass testified that he was not.

Walter Gerash honed in on the fact that Harry Glass was 20 minutes late to work on the day of the robbery and murders. Glass also had no alibi from 9 a.m.-10 a.m. Glass arrived at King Soopers at 11:45 a.m. and that Glass quit the day after the robbery. Harry Glass owned a .357. He lived in Northglenn, Colorado, and was driving into work from home. Glass became emotional when testifying about William McCullom and referred to him as "my friend." Harry Glass had a brother who was a Lewisville police officer, Don Glass. Gerash asked how tall Don Glass was, and Harry Glass looked like he was going to come undone. He answered through gritted teeth that his brother was 5 foot 8. Harry Glass was cleared in the investigation when no one picked him from any of the line-ups.

Mike McKown was a former guard at the United Bank of Denver. He was an alternate suspect. His name was one of the first to be mentioned as a potential suspect. He was 6 feet tall and 190 lbs. In court, he wore a tan suit with a brown vest. He had black hair and a black mustache in court. He was a substitute teacher in Colorado, and he

118   KIMBERLI ROESSING ANDERSON

worked at the United Bank of Denver on the weekends as a
security guard. McKown worked at the bank from February
of 1988 to June of 1990. He trained new guards. McKown
testified that he trained 32 guards in 2-3 years. In the
summer of 1989, he worked with James King, and they
became partners. They were also good friends.

McKown testified that King was "very knowledgeable"
about the bank's security system. He stated that it was a
"bone of contention" as to which one of them knew more
about the system, he or James King. They would challenge
each other. At one point, King challenged McKown to find a
poster of Morgan Fairchild that was somewhere in the bank.
It took Mike McKown a while, but he eventually found it in
a janitor's closet. McKown challenged King to find a snake-
skin that he had seen at the bank. After two months, James
King found it in the atrium. They were friends outside of
work as well.

McKown testified that he owned a .357 Smith & Wesson
revolver, a .9 millimeter semi-automatic, and a .22 automatic. "King preferred to be armed," McKown testified.
McKown described King's gun as old and worn in his court
testimony. McKown had once been assaulted at the auto
bank and wished he had been armed at the time. After the
assault, McKown made sure he was armed at the bank. He
testified that security guard shifts ran from 12p.m. to 12a.m.,
12 a.m. to 12 p.m., and there was a swing shift from 6 a.m. to 6
p.m. McKown testified that the swing shift was a "myth."
"There were never enough guards to have a swing shift," he
said.

Mike McKown's alibi was that he was staying with his
sister, Carol Olsen, in Kent, Washington. The night before
the robbery, he saw a movie with a friend from high school,
Linda Shandy. He slept until 10 a.m. on the morning of the

robbery. He spent the day at his sister's house, waiting for his kids to call because it was Father's Day. There was a call between him and his father from Anaconda, Montana, at some point during the day. His ex-wife called him that night to tell him about the robbery. At some point, his kids called him. Phone records substantiated the calls.

On June 21, 1991, Mike McKown received a letter from James King. King writes about the robbery. At one point in the letter, King wrote that he "felt stuck" because he didn't have a good alibi. Mike and his uncle (who was a prankster) decide to call King on June 24, 1991 and pretend that his uncle was an FBI agent as a joke. The joke fell flat as the FBI had just been to King's house. They only spoke for a few minutes. According to McKown, during that call, King stated that he took his wife to work at Weight Watchers at the Westland Shopping Center on his way to go play chess on Father's Day. McKown testified that Carol King worked weekends. King went back home after not finding anyone at the former chess club, but he told McKown that there had been another man there looking for the chess club too. These statements went different than the statements King had made to investigators, and King denied that he told McKown those things. King also stated that he told McKown that he had taken Carol to work on the day of the phone call and not the day of the robbery.

When the prosecution asked Mike McKown who the robbery sketch looked most like, he testified that it looked most like James King. McKown quit at the bank after the 1990 robbery at the United Bank of Denver. He was cleared by investigators in the 1991 robbery (Denver County, 1992). McKown testified that King had an ankle holster in addition to his gun belt that he wore on duty. McKown looked uncomfortable and sad when he was testifying. King looked much the same. As an observer, I thought it was painful for both of them. McKown had been in town in the weeks before the robbery and had spent time with James King. In a phone call with James Prado after the trial, Mike McKown told Prado that he had suffered a stroke two days after he testified at the James King Trial. It came out in court testimony that McKown had dyed his hair black for the trial and that usually, his hair was salt and pepper in color both on his head and his mustache.

Other men were scrutinized in the three weeks leading up to James King's arrest. Several witnesses and Agent Kirk thought that John Perpetua (a former guard) looked like the sketch. Several of the eye-witnesses picked out John Perpetua as looking somewhat like the suspect. Alibis cleared some, and some took lie detector tests. Others were not cleared until witnesses failed to pick them out of a line-up. Search warrants were served on multiple people. Fifty people were under heavy scrutiny, and that was narrowed to fifteen. King was not on that initial list. It was the sketch created by the FBI based on the witnesses that brought James King into focus. It was the identification process that led to King's arrest.

16
___

W hat the Jury Didn't Know
Jim King was hoping to write a book.
According to several sources, he was writing a
police procedure manual and a fiction novel. What was
returned to him many months after the trial was the start of
a security manual and an outline of a fiction piece. The
pieces were not completed or published and may have been
the musings of a writer who had security and police experience and someone who wanted to write a story. One of his
sons had built him a second-hand computer, and King was
writing. He was using floppy disks to save his work and
putting them in his safety deposit box at the bank. King
thought he could make money as a writer.

Buckley suggested that there was irony in the fact that
while King had a mediocre police career, he thought himself
expert enough to write a book about police procedure. On
the other hand, James King had been trained as a military
policeman and security guard for a nuclear installment in
Germany while in the military. He had a 25-year police
career in a major U.S. city. He had been a security guard at

several different banks and businesses. He may have felt he had something to offer.

Buckley also stated that the fiction piece was salacious, pornographic, and violent. There were instances of people being shot in the back of the head. Buckley argued that these ideas in his working novel were his fantasies. Buckley believed he acted them out during the bank robbery. Buckley wanted King's writings admitted during his trial. The defense argued against the works being introduced to the jury. The judge decided to the split the difference. If the defense opened the door on Jim King's non-violent character, parts of the book might be admitted. The judge was reserving judgment.

There were six false IDs found in James King's safety deposit box at his bank. This is more complicated because while the IDs were not connected to the bank robbery, the fact that the IDs existed at all questioned Jim King's character. For a time, King was the Sergeant of the ID Bureau for DPD. At some point, King made six false ids. He used various forms of his family names and the names of friends: William S. Goody, William J. Keplinger, James W. Ette, James W. King, and Oren W. Marshall. Ette was his biological last name, and Keplinger was his mother's maiden name. King's photo was on all of the IDs. However, the pictures on the IDs were of a younger James King.

Could King have just been playing with the machine? Of course. However, it looks terrible, especially when one is charged with robbery and murder. Making these IDs was against DPD policy, and why would someone need six fake IDs? If someone were playing around, they could have destroyed the IDs, but King kept them in his bank security bank box. Is this proof of criminal intent in some way? Buckley argued to have the IDs introduced into evidence.

The defense argued against it. The judge sided with the defense. The jury never knew about the fake IDs. When DPD returned King's belongings, they refused to return the IDs based on the fact that it was against DPD policy for him to have made them in the first place.

Finally, there was a man who knew James King in the military that the prosecution wanted to add to the witness list. He was an army buddy (Frank Gentry) that claimed that King talked endlessly about how one would rob a bank. Gentry would testify that King was obsessed with it as if it was his favorite hobby. Since the allegations were 37-years-old; Judge Spriggs disallowed Frank Gentry's testimony (Denver County, 1991). The jury never met Frank Gentry.

PART IV

The Interviews

17

T hat Case Still Makes Me Angry
Bill Buckley
District Attorney Norm Early asked Bill
Buckley to take this case, and Lamar Sims and others
assisted him. Speaking with Bill Buckley, I got the sense that
this was the case he never forgot. William P. Buckley started
practicing in 1971. He worked as a prosecutor for 26 years. He
tried 50 murder cases. He was serious about getting justice
for victims. He still looked lawyerly and serious as he sat
across the table from me in an army tee-shirt and jeans at a
local Starbucks. He didn't look 79-years-old. His face was
quite animated, and despite having survived leukemia, he
has perfect hair. His eyes lit up angrily when he spoke about
the case.

Bill Buckley had only planned to be a prosecutor for
about five years. Then, he wanted to go practice law where
he could make some money. However, fate has a way of
changing these things. He received a phone call one day,
and ten hours later, he was standing in his brother's blood in
Yuma, Arizona. His brother, Teddy, was a corrections officer

at a prison there. He had been stabbed 40 times by at least four inmates. He and another corrections officer had been killed. As the eldest of eight children, it fell to Bill to tell the rest of the family. Teddy had a wife and three children, ages two, three, and four-years-old. Bill took responsibility for them.

After his brother's murder, Bill Buckley decided to remain a prosecutor. He could relate to victims and their families because of his own experience. He was able to build a good rapport with victims and their families. He would tell young prosecutors working under him to never tell a victim that they understand what they are going through unless they do. It has always bothered him that he was unable to bring closure to the families of the four slain guards in the United Bank case. (Buckley, 2019)

Bill Buckley does not doubt that James King was the robber of the United Bank Building on June 16, 1991, and the murderer of the four slain guards. Buckley respects the jury's verdict but disagrees wholeheartedly. He blames the loss of the case on the breakdown of the relationship between the Denver Police Department and the FBI. Buckley was very unhappy with the fact that the FBI had shown the vault tellers the guard book photos on June 20. He knew that this would compromise any future line-up that included the guards (Buckley, 2019).

The former prosecutor did not believe that James King had been target shooting at the Federal Reserve Bank Range, noticed that his gun had a cracked cylinder, and then waited for several more months before throwing it away. He scoffed at the idea that King took the gun apart and threw it away in different garbage bags over different days or that King emptied the live ammunition of its gun powder and then tossed the empty shells (Buckley, 2019). King would also claim that he offered his leather holster for that gun to his son and when his son didn't want it, King threw that away too. Buckley pointed out that police policy would have been that King turn in the department issued holster and his two speed loaders when he retired. James King's speed loaders were never found (Buckley, 2019).

Buckley talked about how King had investigated every nook and cranny at United Bank when he worked there. "He went to places he had no business being as a part-time weekend security guard." King studied the security system and had maps of the layout of the bank in his home (In fairness, all of the guards are given these maps when they are hired). Buckley also made the point that during the time James King worked at the bank, there was a camera located in a supervisor's office that recorded the guards in the guard room. During the robbery, attempts were made to enter that office, which was locked. Footprints were left on the plexiglass, and the robber shot at the lock on the door in a vain attempt to get into that office. He was unable to break-in. Buckley felt that King would have wanted to retrieve the VHS tape from that office because he knew there was a camera in there. Ironically, that camera had been moved since King had resigned, and it was located with all of the other cameras in the guard room at the time of the robbery. The robber ended up with the tape anyway (Buckley, 2019).

The mixed ammunition evidence is important. According to Buckley, only a police officer would have had the mixed ammunition from at least four different manufacturers. Only someone in law enforcement would have had mixed ammunition in their firearm. Some of the ammunition from the robbery was police issue only, such as the Federal +P+ ammunition. King had been a Denver Policeman for 25 years. He retired with 18 rounds of ammunition, his service weapon, two speed loaders, and his gun belt. Periodically, the DPD tested new ammunition, and each officer was expected to have the most up to date ammunition in their service weapon. Police officers often kept buckets of mixed ammunition at home where they could dump out the old when new ammunition was issued (Buckley, 2019).

Bill Buckley believes that the reason the robber didn't kill the vault employees was maybe that he was out of ammunition. He may not have expected four guards to be on duty on Father's Day. He might have thought it would have been a skeleton crew. If the robber had six bullets in his gun and two speed loaders that would be eighteen rounds. He may have entered the vault and counting room with an empty weapon and just hoped to get some money and get out alive. According to Buckley, the money was unmarked cash from Saturday night restaurant and bar receipts. This was the money that came in from the armored trucks. Buckley stated that King knew he had to be out by 10 am because, at that time, a group of tellers comes down to the counting room to collect the personal checks from Saturday nights. The robber left the bank at 9:56 am. It was thought that he left the 7th floor of the bank parking garage. There had been some suggestion during the investigation that guards were supposed to park on the 7th floor.

In the aftermath of the robbery, King's actions looked nefarious. The safety deposit box was also an issue, according to Buckley. King had maintained a safety deposit for years, but after the robbery, he requested a larger box. King maintained he was offered a special deal to upgrade the size of the box and that his sons had been after him to get a larger box because they needed room to put car titles and other documents in the box. Buckley believes King got the larger box to store the money from the robbery.

In the days after the robbery, King made several trips to his new larger safety deposit box. Carol was with him on at least one of these trips but stated that she waited outside and smoked a cigarette. When the Denver Police and FBI got into the safety deposit box, there was no money in it. It contained personal papers such as deeds, titles, baptism certificates, birth certificates, among other things. It also contained fake IDs. The box was not full, and there was room for $200k in small bills (Buckley, 2019).

King had testified that one of the reasons he got the larger box was so he could keep computer disks secure. In 1991, computer disks were still quite large. If they were floppy disks, they were even larger. King was writing several manuscripts, including a fiction piece and a police procedure manual. One of his sons had supplied King with a computer he had built and encouraged him to keep the computer disks in a bank box for protection (Gerash & Goodstein, 1997). Buckley felt like the fiction piece was violent and reflected a side of James King the public didn't see. There were scenes where people were shot in the back of the head, much like the four slain guards. King's attorneys argued it was just fantasy and fiction.

Bill Buckley is still in favor of the death penalty. However, in the King case, it forced the burden of proof up 100%. The jury was sequestered during deliberations. Buckley talked about how James King had no reaction when the verdict was read. "He was stoic." An innocent man would have fallen over and been so relieved, but King just stood there with no reaction. I asked Buckley what he thought happened to the robbery money. He pondered that it may have been used to pay his attorneys. There were rumors at the time that the money was buried at Mt. Olivet Cemetery (where Jim and Carol visited later on that Father's Day), and others thought James King had somehow stuffed the money into his roof during a repair project. However, the Denver Police checked these places and many more. The robbery money was never found. The FBI kept watching over James King and his family for years after the robbery (Robinson, 2019).

AUTHOR'S NOTE

William P. Buckley is the kind of public servant that we all should strive to be. Born in Midland, Texas, on March 1, 1940, he is the eldest of eight children. His mother had six boys and then later, two girls. Bill went to Regis for three years but realized there were too many siblings in college at the same time. He took a year off to work. He was drafted to Vietnam. He never had to leave the United States, though, because he has a beautiful singing voice and became part of the "Singing Chorus." They traveled 64, 000 miles in one year. He married an army nurse and, over the years, had three children. Buckley had hoped to use the GI Bill to finish school, but it had expired. He ended up working and going to law school at Denver University at night. All the while, he continued singing at various clubs and piano bars.

Bill worked in the DA's office for 26 years and tried 50 murder cases (none with the advanced technology of DNA). The murder of his brother, Teddy (a corrections officer in Arizona), affected him deeply, and this is the reason he remained a prosecutor for so long. The United Bank Robbery case also affected him profoundly, and he said that he didn't take good care of himself or issues with his wife and family in the aftermath. Buckley was also a defense attorney for an additional 19 years. In 2006, Bill was diagnosed with leukemia, and luckily one of his younger sisters was a match for him. He married his second wife around the same time. He met her at the "Whispers" piano bar. She was a secretary for the ICU at Swedish Hospital.

In 2013, Bill was hit by a car and suffered some severe injuries. Despite all that, he has participated in a lifetime of public service. Throughout his life, he has been on several boards, including Denver Victims Service Center (14 years), Leukemia/Lymphoma Society (12 years),; St. Anthony Flight for Life Advisory Committee (8 years). Bill raised money for the cost of the program: and because it was the first of its kind, others came to visit and modeled their program after it. Bill's second wife died in 2015. He said that they took care of each other. Bill Buckley is now completely retired and enjoying his life.

Photo by Kimberli Roessing-Anderson, 2019
Bill Buckley with his little red corvette

18

J uror 502

Leaving Colorado

Dorothy Stevenson was one of the jurors summoned to hear James King's trial in 1992. She was a hold out along with one of the male jurors for a conviction. She changed her mind about a day before the jury settled on a verdict. Dorothy worked at United Airlines in the kitchen at the time of the trial. "No, nothing ever came out after the trial to make me change my mind." She said during our phone interview. She considered the experience "pretty traumatic." Dorothy was a hold out on the jury because she felt as though there were "too many coincidences." "James King had shaved his mustache off, he admitted being downtown at the time of the robbery, he threw away his gun, and he got a bigger bank box." She said. She thought that the problem was that the case was all circumstantial.

The issue that bothered Dorothy the most was that James King's service revolver disappeared. She thought it odd that police offer that had served for so long would throw away his gun. Dorothy stated that one of the things that turned her around to an acquittal was that there was no smell of gun powder on the suspect. She had been moved by an expert witness that testified about the aroma of gun powder being absent in the vault and counting room.

"There was just no way to convict," she said. There was no "physical evidence" that tied James King to the crime. The experience was also traumatic because some of her co-workers from United Airlines had come forward to the judge and stated that Dorothy was a biased juror. They said that she had made strong comments about Jim King being guilty before she was called as a juror. Dorothy was then sternly questioned by the judge. The judge subpoenaed five of her co-workers and questioned them. Deliberations were suspended. She remained on the jury but found the trial and deliberations to be stressful. Dorothy had also been misinterpreted by someone in the media as stating that she was a supervisor at United Airlines. This misinformation made its way into the press. Dorothy says she never said that, and it caused issues with her co-workers when she returned to work.

In the aftermath of the trial, she went back to work and tried to move on. She stated that the media camped out on her neighborhood corner for several weeks after the trial. In 1994, United Airlines sold its food service, and Dorothy decided to move to Kansas. She wanted to spend some time with her aging mother before her mother passed away. Dorothy got a year with her. She has had no contact with the jury after the trial. "I moved away and put the trial out of my mind" As far as she knew, no one kept in contact from the jury. Freshly divorced, she also moved to Kansas so she wouldn't run into her ex-husband at the grocery store each week. Dorothy said he lived only a mile away from her at the time. She joined the YMCA and two quilting clubs in Kansas, and she was happy. Her sister still lives in the same town. Dorothy says that because she doesn't live in Colorado anymore, she never hears about the case.

Dorothy and her son were recently back in Denver for her ex-husband's funeral. She could not believe how much the city had grown and how bad the traffic was now. She doesn't regret moving to Kansas. Dorothy stated that the traffic was so bad that they didn't even stop in town to visit. They attended the funeral in Denver and immediately returned to Kansas.

19

Wesn't Allowed to Take Notes
Juror 222
Thomas Brunn was a juror in the King
case, and he believes that if there had been the forensics
advancements that we have today; the case would have been
solved. Fresh from a tour of the Denver Crime Lab with his
wife and friends, he was impressed with the facility. Tom
wondered if the money from the robbery had ever been
found. When I was interviewing him, he said that he felt
like the investigation honed in on James King too soon and
that others might have been involved. Brunn doesn't believe
that one person could have covered that much ground in
that short amount of time with his neighbors seeing King at
10 a.m. in his yard.

Having said that, Tom thought that King was either
guilty or a very unlucky person. He thought it was a mistake
that jurors were not allowed to take notes during the trial.
The firearms testimony was too much and too detailed to
remember. "There was all of this testimony about the gun
powder, and it was just too much to remember." He said.

There was much made of the safety deposit box. Nothing was incriminating in the safety deposit box, according to Brunn. "Not enough evidence." He said.

The attitude of the jurors was, "Let's get this over with!" They had been sequestered for nine days. "Thank God it wasn't the whole trial," Brunn stated. "The jury selection took a week." While foreperson, Joni Haack had told People Magazine back in 1992 that there was only one vote in the jury room on the day of the verdict, Tom doesn't remember it that way. He remembers passing the paper around with people discussing "issues" and then passing the note on to the next juror. He remembers the media barraging the jurors at the courthouse when they tried to exit. Almost all the jurors had media camped out at their homes.

Tom credits Scott Robinson with the disguise and overlay exhibits. He stated that they were essential in the case. "They were very effective." He said. He also remembers being creeped out by the Styrofoam heads with the "Knitting Needles" sticking out of them that the prosecution presented. He thought it was disturbing. He thought too much was made of the firearms testimony, and the "very bad" novel King was writing. "It was about whether King did or didn't do it." He said. He noted that King's wife, Carol, was there every day. He stated that if he had been accused of a crime that he would hope that family and friends would be that supportive.

Tom explained that the jury was diverse, and that was a good thing. This kept anyone from being ganged upon. The jury was not concerned with it being a death penalty case but rather whether or not King was the person who did it. He remembers being taken to the state capitol when the judge was speaking with the juror (Dorothy Stevenson). They were dismissed until the ordeal was worked out. Tom never thought Dorothy seemed biased against King in the jury room. Tom remembers thinking it odd that guard (Bill McCullom) had family members that came in and cleaned out his apartment the day after the robbery. He thought that was weird. The family cleaned it out the very next day. He also remembered that McCullom had security documents in his front shirt pocket when he was found.

Tom never knew about the false I.D.s that James King had in his safety deposit box. The judge ruled that evidence inadmissible, and he never heard about them after the trial. He guessed that the fake I.D.s could have been made as part of a getaway plan. The other items, such as King's writings and such he didn't think would have made a difference to the jury. "King either did or didn't do it." He added that there was no direct evidence. It was all circumstantial.

Thomas R. Brunn was born in Ohio. He spent time in Delaware and Wisconsin. He would have stayed in Madison, but at the time, they had no architecture school. He ended up in Boulder at Colorado University for architecture school. He liked the weather and decided to stay in Colorado. He has been called for jury duty once since the King trial. He was chosen, but the case was settled. He was glad because, as he said it, "I've done my time."

20

Not Proven

Juror 460

Jack A Rushin was a juror in the James King case. "There should be three choices," said Jack Rushin in our interview. Guilty, Not Guilty, and Not Proven." Rushin explained that he pushed several of the jurors to their verdicts. He often sat beside the foreperson (Joni Haack), and she would have to tell him to let others speak. "I found out that I am a pretty persuasive person." He said. Jack stated that the jury was very close to being hung. Several jurors were saying that they needed a break, but Jack was insistent that they deliberate through the weekend. He was afraid if they took a break, they would not be able to reach a verdict.

He pushed Dorothy Stevenson (who was the second to last hold-out). She was unsure of herself. According to Jack, she told him that the jury should find James King guilty and let Gerash get him off on appeal. Let it be his problem. Rushin explained to her that it was the jury's job to decide guilty or not guilty. Jack said that she seemed overwhelmed. He said that the quarters were tight, and people had to slide behind each other to get around the room or go to the bathroom. A female juror named Valarie Taylor would sit on a ledge on the second floor to escape for a few minutes. This made Jack nervous, and he would tell her to get down off of there. Valarie explained that there was too much pressure, and she couldn't handle it.

Jack didn't find the testimony complicated. He felt that there was more than one person involved. He always thought it was one of the guards that was involved. "Two hundred thousand isn't a lot to split between two people." He said. He had some issues with the firearms testimony on cross-examination. Jack stated that 2 of the 3 FBI agents testified that there was more lead weight than 18 rounds. This would mean that more than 18 rounds were fired, but no one could explain that. He also thought that the robber would have to have a vast knowledge of the bank's security system.

He found King's testimony to be flat and guarded. He was very even, not charming. "I didn't like the guy. I thought he did it." He said. Rushin wasn't sure if it was about the money. He thought possibly that King just wanted to prove that he could do it. It bothered him that one of King's police partners had testified about an incident where King stayed locked in the patrol car while his partner was involved in a bar brawl. There was also an incident where King fired in the air to stop an armed subject as opposed to shooting the suspect. Jack thought that the prosecution was trying to show that James King didn't follow the rules. Jack wishes the jury could have questioned James King after the lawyers were done.

Jack thought that Judge Spriggs did an excellent job but felt like the prosecution and the defense were like used car salesmen. "I didn't believe the prosecution. I didn't believe the defense either." He said. He didn't believe the chess alibi to be unbelievable, and he thought it was possible that King's service weapon had a cracked cylinder, and he deposed of it. Jack thought too much was made of the attachment to a gun. He said that if he had been in a war and killed people, he wouldn't want to keep the weapon. He has a gun that his father handed down to him, and that means something to him because it was his father's gun.

Jack wasn't impressed with the overlays or the witness identification expert. Still, on the other hand, the prosecution wasn't proving that James King did it. In the jury room, according to Jack, the moles were a big issue. James King had a lot of moles and several prominent ones on his face. The jury found it interesting that not even David Barranco (who stood beside King for several minutes) noticed the moles. David was filling the black bag with money in the vault. Most of the victims had described the robber as having a clear complexion. The moles became a big part of the jury discussion.

There was a lot of compassion for Nina McGinty among the jurors. Jack described her as frantic on the stand. Nina was the teller that hid behind a counter and wastebasket during the robbery. She was there until the police found her after the robbery. She had to be hospitalized. According to Jack, she was so traumatized. "She sobbed on the stand the whole time." He said. "Other witnesses were emotional but not like Nina." The defense team came after her hard because Nina was the only witness that picked, James King, out of the six-man photo line-up that had not been previously shown the guard book. Nina testified that as she was bending down behind the counter, she got a look at his face for a few seconds.

Jack talked about touring the bank with the jury during the trial. "Somebody did this horrible thing, but who did it?' he asked. The robber had no blood or blood spatter on him. "Why would James King use his police revolver to rob the bank when he had other firearms? His police revolver was easily traceable?" He asked. Jack said that one of the female jurors who had worked for the fire department told the jury that there was a lot of pressure to find someone and try them for this crime. However, there was no direct evidence, according to Jack, and it was all circumstantial. Jack also disputes the jury's foreperson's assertion that there was only one vote in the jury room. About King's testimony, Jack stated the defense attorneys had him trained.

He stated that the jury voted many times. He remembers the first vote being 9/3 for a guilty verdict. He joined the not guilty side because he was afraid there was going to be a conviction before there was even any discussion. After the verdict, he was terrified that if the jury were polled, someone would change their mind. Jack said that he made Dorothy cry a few times, and other jurors got on his case. "Prove to me that King committed this crime." He said. He described the last hold-out as a "wild card." He remembered him being possibly an airline mechanic and younger. Jack said that he acted standoffishly and would state that he didn't want to talk when it was his turn to speak to the jury. Jack noted that he acted oddly on the phone during phone and visitation time. Jack was surprised when the last hold-out finally gave-in.

Jurors were feeling other stress, as well. According to Jack, one of the female jurors was having problems with her boss at work. Her boss was pressuring her to find a way to get off the jury. He wanted her back at work. He was threatening to fire her. She was upset and spoke to Jack about it. Jack told her to tell one of the two bailiffs. The female juror did speak with one of the bailiffs (Frank), who then took the allegation to the judge. Judge Spriggs' office reached out to the employer and offered to bring him in and explain how "this" works. The employer declined, and there were no other issues with that juror and her job.

Jack Rushin had tried not to get on the James King jury. "I sat near him during jury selection and just stared at him (King)." Finally, the bailiff told Jack to knock it off and that he knew what he was doing. Jack prides himself on being a good listener, and he had Lamar Sim's questions memorized by the time he juror number was called. "I just started answering, "Yes, No, No, Yes." Sims stopped him and asked him to wait for the question. He got picked despite these efforts. When asked about being a juror, Jack said, "It took a lot out of me."

Since the trial, Jack has been interviewed by local TV stations on anniversaries and was part of a six-person panel of jurors that appeared on Dateline after the trial. He ran into Bill Buckley on the street once, and they had a lively discussion about the weight of the lead left at the crime scene. He also spoke to the judge about the case. According to Jack, Judge Spriggs said that Gerash kept them in pre-motions for nearly a year to keep out certain potential evidence.

Jack is an electrical contractor and has done work on the United Bank building and for Lamar Sims since the trial. Jack thought Sims had a big ego. Sims wasn't friendly. He brought up the case with Sims, who was visibly upset by the mention of it. Jack said that he understood why Sims was upset because a lot of effort went into the case. Jack and

Thomas Brunn happened to attend the same church for a while at Mile High Church in Lakewood, but most of the jurors did not keep in contact. When I asked him if the fact that this was a death penalty case made a difference to him, Jack said, "If King had been found guilty and the prosecution had proven it then "Fry Him."

21

V ery Happy with My Decision
Juror 336

REZA R. Jalini was a juror on the James. King case. "I am very happy with my decision." Reza explained that it was "torturous" being a juror on the King case. He said that the last hold-out was an unemployed guy who was happy making $50 a day on jury duty. Jalini (who has worked in radiology) was losing money. There was a week of jury selection, a three- week trial, and nine days of deliberation. In deliberation, the jurors were sequestered. The trial caused him a lot of stress.

The evidence was all circumstantial, according to Jalini. There was no direct evidence. He felt that there was just as much evidence against Paul Yocum. During our interview, he mentioned Paul Yocum several times. He stated that there was talk about Yocum in the jury room. Reza also said there was a lot of discussion about the death penalty. "The death penalty aspect just made it worse." When asked if he was impressed with the firearms testimony by the prosecution or the overlay presentation by the defense, Jalini stated that the trial was just a game to the attorneys. "Lawyers made a game of competing experts and props."

Reza thought Gerash and Robinson were great attorneys. "There were much more powerful," he said. As for the testimony regarding the "mixed ammunition," he said that anyone preparing to commit a crime such as this one would have done some planning and research first. He felt like King was arrested too soon. "The state has a lot of power to accuse someone." He said. Reza thought that there was politics involved in arresting someone quickly to satisfy the public. Reza is at peace with his decision not to convict because he is not sure King committed the crime, and there was no DNA, fibers, fingerprints, or other forensic evidence.

Reza had a heart attack two years after the trial ended. He attributes some of that stress leading up to the heart attack to the trial. "The trial was very stressful." He said. He contradicts the jury foreperson, who stated that there was only one vote. Reza noted that there was a lot of back and forth. Jalini indicated that in the beginning, several jurors thought that King was guilty. He said that the jury room was cramped and small. Jalini pointed out that a jury had never been out for nine days before. They deliberated for 53 hours. He stated that the jury didn't need to go through all of the evidence again, but they did it anyway.

Reza was bothered by the constant presence of police officers or the bailiff. The jurors each had their hotel room. They were not allowed to visit each other. During meals, a police officer sat with them. There was no TV in his room. He couldn't read the paper. Any contact with his wife was monitored. She brought him clothes during the deliberations, but he couldn't speak with her. Jalini said that a police officer stayed on their hotel floor. Sometimes, some of the jurors would go for a walk for exercise, but a police officer had to go with them.

They were not allowed to speak of the case unless they were in the jury room, which he understood, but he didn't like being sequestered. "I felt like I was the one in jail." He said. "Jurors bring their personal stuff into the jury room." He said. "I came in with an open mind." Some people brought their religion, bias, and some didn't understand reasonable doubt or other concepts about being a juror, according to Jalini. He stated that he was miserable and couldn't wait to get the trial over with and done.

Since the trial, Reza has had heart surgery, stints, and is still on medication. His wife told him that he was not the same person after the trial. Reza didn't keep in touch with anyone from the jury. "I never think about the case. I have no regrets." He said. He meditates and tries to avoid stress. He is an avid reader and spend a lot of time doing that and trying to relax. He has been called for jury duty but finds a way to get out of it. "I have done my part," he said.

We spoke a little bit about the death penalty. Reza doesn't believe in it now. He thinks prison is a much more effective punishment. "Death is too easy." He said. He also believes that too many people have been released from prison based on DNA evidence. He is afraid an innocent person could be put to death. "You don't want to kill a guy and then have it be the wrong guy." He said. He also feels that attorneys on both sides set out to pick jurors that they could easily manipulate. "Also, a defendant's ability to hire a good attorney makes a difference to the defense he receives," he said.

22

The Feeling Never Goes Away

David Barranco was the principal witness for the prosecution. He began working for United Bank in September of 1990. "Jim King did it," David told me during our interview. He said that ten or eleven seconds of seeing his face stays with him forever. "Time heals all wounds, but that ten seconds or so stays with me." David believes the case will never be solved because James King was found not guilty. David doesn't believe the robbery was just about the money. He thinks it was about proving he (the robber) could do it and not get caught. The robber left over two million dollars behind in the adjacent vault.

David worried that King would seek revenge on him for testifying or that there was a second robber who might come after him. He remembered being shown 15-20 photos from a guard yearbook on June 20, 1991. David didn't want to point the finger at anyone and get them in trouble, but he wishes now that he would have. David says that he recognized James King in the guard book but didn't want to say anything. He believes the case would have been a lot easier if he had told the FBI right then. Barranco says that the robbery was a very "traumatic event."

David stated that he felt violated. The robber took him to each teller station and had him put money in the small bag, which David describes as being no larger than a zip-up case that a man might put his toiletries in when he traveled. He said there wasn't panic and the robber didn't yell. It was robotic. The robber gave him instructions, and David followed them. David thought that all of the tellers were on the ground in the mantrap. It wasn't until he entered Nina McGinty's desk area that he saw her legs and realized she was hiding behind the wastebasket. David had to remain calm and pretend he had not seen her, and he just kept moving. He said that Nina was in the worst shape after the robbery, and she had to be hospitalized. She was in complete shock after the incident. Nina wasn't able to stand up and walk when the police found her. She was hysterical and screaming.

"My gut knew him in the courtroom," said David about James King. David also believes someone had to be helping him. How could he have gotten ten VHS tapes, ammunition, shell casings, a two-way radio, log sheets from the blue logbook, and the money in that small zipper case? David wondered if it was another guard or even a family member. "There had to be someone else," he said.

Sadly, David recollected seeing Phillip Mankoff and Scott McCarthy near the vault about 30-45 minutes before the robbery. Mankoff was taking McCarthy on a tour as it was McCarthy's first day on the job. Everyone waved or acknowledged each other, and the guards moved on with less than an hour to live. Fate dealt a cruel hand to several people that day. It was McCarthy's first day on the job. David

Barranco had filled in for a co-worker that day so that the co-worker could have Father's Day off to be with his family.

David didn't usually work the half shift on Sundays. He is thankful that he and the others in the counting room didn't hear the shots or know that the robber had killed the four guards when he came into the counting room. He doesn't feel that they could have been calm or kept it together if they had known. I asked Barranco if he thought he was going to die that day, and he said, "Yeah, I did." When David had put enough money in the bag, the robber told him to join the others in the mantrap. He did. There were two mantraps. The vault tellers were stuck in one mantrap, and the robber went back out the other mantrap using a pass card from one of the murdered guards.

Trapped in the mantrap, one of the tellers found a metal spoon, according to Barranco, and the group began trying to pry open the door. Once they freed themselves, they used a rear exit to find some other security guards and call the police. In the meantime, different departments had been trying to get ahold of the four slain guards with no response, and panic was starting to descend on the bank.

David suffered six months of nightmares and developed PTSD. He strongly disagreed with the bank policy that rid security guards of their firearms. In the aftermath, the bank offered mental health counseling to the vault tellers, and David accepted that help. He also moved to another department. He wasn't thrilled with the case being aired on Court TV even though his face had been blurred it when he testified. He can't explain why he didn't notice the moles on James King. He stated that he could see them clearly in the courtroom from far away. He said that moles were distinct and covered his face. David didn't understand why someone with that many moles wouldn't just wear a hood that covered his face. He wondered if the disguise and the face bandage were not an attempt to distract witnesses from seeing the moles. Also, the robber told the employees (several times) not to look at his face.

David said he was riding up an elevator at work when someone told him that James King had been found "Not Guilty." He went into shock again. All of the feelings came back. David had been the first witness to work with the FBI sketch artist. He had been closest to the robber and spent the most time with him. The other witnesses had just added and subtracted from that original sketch. David was only 24-years-old at the time of the robbery and second-guessed some of his decisions, such as not telling the FBI that he recognized James King from the guard book. He also thought that security was "not great" at the bank at the time of the robbery, and he should have resigned when the guards were first told they couldn't carry firearms anymore. I asked David if he thought he had ever met King while working at the bank and doesn't remember ever meeting him.

One of the issues that frustrated David the most was the quality of all of the photos. He said the photos in the guard book were too small (like little yearbook photos), and the quality was horrible. He also noted that the quality of the pictures in the six-man line-up (over the July 4th holiday) wasn't any better. David said that all of the black "bags" police and the FBI showed him before the trial were too large. It wasn't a briefcase, duffel bag, or even a satchel. Everything he was shown was too big. David tried to explain what type of bag it was, but no one seemed to understand what he meant. He thought it was similar to a toiletry bag with a zipper down the middle.

David left the bank in 1993. He went back to Phoenix,

where he had more family support. He had not wanted his parents to know how bad of shape he was in or what he was experiencing, but he finally acknowledged that he needed their help. David also spoke to me about June 16 of 2019 being the 28th anniversary of the robbery. He said it was a bad day, and he always thinks about the robbery on Father's Day. He recently lost his father, so this year was more difficult. He is sad that the slain guard's families never got justice or closure. David says that even today, he thinks about his bank being robbed while he is conducting his private bank business. *The feeling never goes away.*

D avid Saw Him First
    David saw him first. David Twist was in a
    back cage counting money with fellow teller,
Chung Choe when he saw the profile of the man he says was
James King turn a corner. He was someone that didn't
belong in that area of the bank two levels below the ground
floor. "It was suspicious and weird," David said to me during
our interview. "I told David Barranco (the supervisor) and
then tried to follow the man to get a better look." "Suddenly,
the robber came around another corner and was pointing a
gun at us." "It was James King," Twist stated without a
doubt. He remembers identifying him from the guard book,
although the FBI agent testified that no one identified James
King from the guard book on June 20th. Twist identified
James King in court.

    David stated that nothing has happened since the trial
to change his mind about who he saw holding the gun on
that Father's Day of 1991. He is sure of his identification.
Twist stated that he was confident when looking at the six-
man photo line-up he was shown on that July 4th holiday

back in 1991. David described the robber as calm but deliberate. He ordered everyone but Barranco into one of the
mantrap. David said that he and Choe were believers in God
and hit the floor, praying. At some point, he realized Nina
McGinty wasn't with them, and he didn't know what had
happened to her. He didn't realize until later that she had
been hiding.

David believed it was "Divine Intervention" that saved
them. I asked Twist if he thought the robber was going to
kill him. "I don't know," he said, "You never know what is in
someone's head." David felt that the robber wasn't as threatened by the tellers as he had been the guards. "He knew he
had the upper hand." He said. He described the black bag
the robber was carrying like a briefcase. He didn't think it
was a small travel case (as David Barranco did). Twist
believes it was more like a briefcase, but he wasn't 100%
sure.

David worked with law enforcement to try and
remember details about the robber. He had a general recog-
nition, but the gun had become the focal point of his
memory. David described the gun as six feet wide and tall.
He had to work around that to remember what the robber
looked resembled. Twist didn't remember any moles. He
remembered the hat and the sunglasses and the general
look. When he saw the six-man line-up, he recognized King
immediately. He said he never had to consider the other
evidence such as the mustache, the gun, or the bank box
because he saw King and knew it was King.

David was traumatized by the fact that after the robbery,
the police and FBI took the vault tellers back into the bank
to interview them. It was then that the tellers were told that
three of the guards had been murdered. The suspect had
not been caught. "They shouldn't have brought us back in

there." David said, "Why would they take us in there when they had not caught the suspect yet?" David explained that it shook them up to be back in the bank after the robbery. It wasn't until later that the tellers found out about the 4th guard being killed.

When David found out about the verdict, he thought it was because the case was circumstantial, and there was no physical evidence to link King to the crimes. "He got off," David said. Twist feels that the disarming of the bank before the robbery was "Stupid." "How can the guards secure the bank without having lethal force?" he asked. David had started at the bank about a year before the robbery and stayed about a year afterward. He was given the choice of transferring to another department following the robbery, which he decided to do. He transferred to the check processing department. He joked that no gets killed over checks.

Twist didn't watch the trial on Court TV, and he wasn't allowed (as a witness) to sit on testimony. He stated that a police officer brought him in to testify and took him out when he was finished. He knew that the money the robber took was not marked. He said the marked money was in another vault. Twist stated that he thought about 144k was missing with two million left behind. The robber wanted 20's, 50's, and 100's. David was glad that the tellers didn't know about the guards being killed before the robbery. He wasn't sure they could have remained calm if they had known that the robber had just killed four people. About 20 minutes after the robber left, the tellers started trying to get help and get out of the mantrap. One of the women (according to David) found a metal spoon and began trying to force open the door.

One odd thing that happened before the robbery was

that one of the guards, Phillip Mankoff, walked through the vault area with a new guard (Scott McCarthy). He introduced the new guard to everyone, and then they moved on. Twist said that this had never happened before. In all the time he had worked for the bank, he had never had a conversation with a guard. Those two guards were killed about a half an hour after they walked through the vault area. This was also shocking for the tellers to learn. Twist is still bewildered that the guards were unarmed.

About 28 years after the robbery, David said that "You don't get over it, but you move on." He explained that for about 4-5 years, it changed his views and his approach to life. Eventually, he moved on. David stated that his life has been really good. Twist never worked for another bank. David is a strong supporter of the 2nd Amendment. He believes guards and police officers should be able to use lethal force to do their jobs. He has had his own IT company for about 18 years. He is happy and healthy.

The Wilson Family Remembers Todd

Todd Wilson, picture
courtesy of the Wilson Family, 2019

. . .

THE MEDIA REPORTED that Todd was blind in one eye. He was not. He was born with Nystagmus in both eyes, which causes rapid eye movement and severe lazy eye in his right eye. According to the American Optometric Association, *Nystagmus is a vision condition in which the eyes make repetitive, uncontrolled movements. These movements often result in reduced vision and depth perception and can affect balance and coordination.* Todd underwent surgery at 18 months to correct the lazy eye. He was diagnosed as legally blind as the Nystagmus could not be repaired. He attended the school for the blind in North Dakota until the third grade.

When Todd was ten-years-old, the family moved to Colorado to be closer to family. Todd's sister, Tawnya, remembers being the irritating little sister that bugged her brothers and tattled on them, but Todd was always there for her. Todd was close to all of his siblings. "Family was very important to Todd." She said. According to Todd's mother, DeLila, Todd was everything you could ask, for he had a great sense of humor, a big kind caring heart always willing to help if asked. "Even with all his struggles, he always tried to stay positive & never complained about his vision problems but compensated as needed to get through everyday stuff." She said.

Sports were not easy for Todd, but he played one year of football in high school. He loved to watch sports. Todd was in the band and played the tuba and bass. Todd & Scott (Scott McCarthy was one of the other guards murdered that day) worked together at Mission Trujillo as dishwashers through high school, and they became best friends almost right away. Todd was the best man at Scott's wedding. It was at Mission Trujillo where the boys got their nicknames Loco Oho and Gabby (crazy eye due to his issues & gabby because Scott didn't talk much).

When Todd graduated from high school, he worked and later started college at Metro State to become an alcohol and drug counselor. Todd started working at the bank as a file clerk, and when Norwest bought United and the policy for security guards to be armed was changed, he decided to take the security guard position so he could study in the downtime. He said he felt guilty that he was able to study while he was getting paid. Later, Scott McCarthy would also apply to work at the bank with Todd. On the day of the robbery, Scott was being trained by Phillip Mankoff. According to Tawnya, when we found out what happened, we were at my grandparents' house for Father's Day. "We had the news on and saw it. My parents were late getting there, so they walked into a very dismal house. We tried to contact Todd, the bank, and we had a family friend that worked for the bank, so we called him. We got no response. My brother (Trent) drove down to the bank to see if he could get anyone to talk to him, but he was turned away. We didn't find out what had happened to Todd and Scott until like 7 pm that night. "They sent officers and a representative from the bank to the house to tell us. By this time, we pretty much knew what had happened, but it was still a shock to actually hear it." From there, Trent and I went with the police to try and find Jennifer (Scott McCarthy's wife)." My parents stayed with family." She said.

According to Tawnya, as far as the trial went, she tried to go to it even though her parents asked her not to go. "I saw King come around the corner, and I almost passed out, and just past his head, I saw my dad's face." She said.

Her dad went into the courtroom with her. She stated that King sat there with no expression on his face, no remorse, no guilt he wouldn't even look our direction. Tawnya said that was all she could take; she never went back to court. Her mother did her best to watch it on TV. They recorded it, but she wasn't sure any of them really ever made it through the entire thing. They mainly watched it on the news & got the day to day happenings. Her father (John) went to the trial in person.

"I don't believe that any of our minds have changed as far as his guilt goes; he did this, but we believe there was more involved to all this. We have always believed that it was more than just King but have never believed it was another guard. The bank did nothing to try and determine what really happened. Was it because of the recent merger? Was it because it was an election year, and they just wanted this to go away? We don't' know, but they did nothing for the families to help in the investigation or to get any closure for any of us. The fact that there were four guards that day never even got brought up, there were usually only two or three. Scott was training for his first day, which would have been on Monday." Tawnya said.

"Our family and I am sure all the families involved will never going to be the same, so pointless and evil, no closure, no answers for anything how do you resume a normal life after something like that? Answers don't bring them back, but it helps with closure; instead, we all have this void that will always be there. We have no contact with any of Todd's friends. I think it is way too painful for everyone." Tawnya explained.

"My brother was an amazing person and would have done great things if given the chance." She said. Tawnya explained that the family misses Todd every day. I wish he was alive to meet my children, but that was taken from me. "We will probably never know by who or why, and we deal with that every day." She said. Tawnya wonders why the news can do all these cold case stories and podcasts, but no one really ever tried to solve this case for some reason.

Todd Wilson kept his personal life pretty under wraps; he was dating someone when this happened but only for a few months. Todd loved to go fishing and would go every chance he got, even if it was only for a few hours. Todd and Scott McCarthy would go to the mountains on weekends to fish, four-wheel, and have fun. Tawnya said that Todd wanted "as many children as he could afford. He would have been a great uncle and father."

*Todd, Trent and Tawnya have an older brother (Kevin) not pictured) from on their father's side of the family.

1. Todd, Tawnya, and Trent Wilson, (2) Todd
   Wilson
2. John, DeLila, and Todd Wilson
3. Pictures, courtesy of the Wilson Family, 2019

25

Brother Remembers
Scott McCarthy

TODD WITH SCOTT , 1990
   Courtesy, Cody McCarthy, 2019
   According to Cody (Scott's brother), Scott hoped that

working as a security guard would help him become a
police officer. Born in Anacortes, Washington, on March 3,
1970, Scott Raymond McCarthy was the middle son of three
sons to Sharon McCarthy. By the time Scott was in junior
high school, the family had moved to Colorado to be closer
to family. Scott attended Heritage High School, where he
met Todd Wilson. They became best friends. They worked
together at Mission Trujillo. It was at Mission Trujillo where
the boys got their nicknames Loco Oho and Gabby (crazy
eye due to his issues & gabby cause Scott didn't talk much).

Scott and Todd in high school
Courtesy, Ancestry, 2019

Courtesy, Cody McCarthy, 2019
Scott served his country in the Army (military police) for

two years. Scott was stationed at Ft. McClellan, Alabama. He was honorably discharged with a shoulder and lower back injury. "He returned home to pursue becoming a police officer," Cody said. Todd Wilson hooked him up with the security job at the United Bank of Denver. Scott was supposed to start on Monday, but Todd asked him to come in on Sunday (the day of the robbery), so he could show him around and do a walkthrough. That is why Scott didn't have on a uniform. Scott was the only guard to fight back. According to Cody, they could tell because the mace/pepper spray had been sprayed, and Scott was shot in the hand as he tried to defend himself.

Scott was a quiet person, according to his brother. "He had a huge heart for helping others, and he was always a protector of friends and family." This is most likely why he was drawn to police/security work. Scott played football in high school. He enjoyed the outdoors. Scott liked scenic drives and fishing. At the same time, he worked at Mission Trujillo; he also worked at Auto Wash on County Line and Holly. "Our family fell apart after Scott died. My mother moved away, and then she passed away. I never knew my dad, and I have raised myself since I was about sixteen." Cody has Scott's military tags, and he wears them almost every day.

On August 4, 1990, Scott married Jennifer Ann McElhaney of Littleton, Colorado. They

had dated during their high school years and attended prom together.

Todd Wilson was the best man. The Wilson family is aso pained because Todd brought Scott into the security job. It was by chance the Scott was even there that day. His first official day should have been on Monday. He was training with Phillip Mankoff in the hours leading up to the robbery.

His mother-in-law, Lawreen McElhaney, stated, "He was the best son-in-law you could ask for. He treated my daughter like a princess." (Daily Sentential, 1991). The Wilson and McCarthy families were close and held double funerals for both men on June 19, 1991, three days after the murders (Daily Sentential, 1991). His mother-in-law was very outspoken after the "Not Guilty" verdict. She felt that the jury did not get the entire story. Scott was remembered with a beautiful headstone, but that is no way to have to remember someone who was only 21-years-old.

COURTESY, Ancestry, 2019

I will also be haunted by the crime scene photo of Scott McCarthy. His huge cowboy boots take over the picture. This is a reminder that it was his first day. He was training and didn't have his uniform yet. According to family, this was a job he was excited about, and he was gunned down. In the hour before his death, and Phillip Mankoff was seen by vault employees touring the bank. Scott was seen smiling and waving at the vault tellers. That memory has remained with the vault tellers that I interviewed for this book.

How Scott McCarthy was shot indicates that he turned and faced his killer after Phillip Mankoff was executed. Scott did not go like a lamb to the slaughter. He turned around, stuck his hand out, and tried to defend himself. Possibly, some DNA from the killer got on his clothes, something that was not able to be detected in 1991 or 1992. Scott McCarthy, Jennifer, and his brothers deserve justice just as all of the victims and survivors do.

26

J ennifer's Memories in Pictures

Courtesy, Jennifer Rios, 2019

JENNIFER WAS MARRIED to Scott McCarthy for less than a year when he was murdered. They had dated in high school and attended prom. They were married on August 4, 1990. Jennifer stated that Scott wanted children. Jennifer remembers Scott as loving, attentive, and forgiving. She attended the trial but was not there for the verdict. She did not think she could handle it. Her parents were there for it and she stayed with family. About James King, she said, "He was inconsiderate. It was hard to see him and I'm sure I wanted to pass out. I had to walk passed him one day when we left the courtroom. He looked at his wife, who was right behind me. He literally said, " kiss kiss, baby." To her. I was right there. It took everything I had not to react. It was a good thing there was a separating wall."

"There was a day when I was in the courtroom when they were describing how the guards were killed step by step. At one point, I was going to burst out in tears. I stopped breathing because if I did, it was going to be a loud cry. I barely made it to the hallway and gasped. I trusted our court system at the time. I believed in the process. I really didn't know much about the jury." She said. Jennifer was with her Aunt Brenda when she heard the verdict.

Jennifer remembers the day of the robbery painfully. "I worried about him." She said. "He was good about checking in, and I had not heard from him." Jennifer knew something was wrong before she heard anything. She felt it. It was intuition. She had felt it even the day before. "I first found out what happened that day on the news." She said that the names of the victims were not released because families had not been notified. Jennifer explained that because it was Scott's first day on the job, she did know his exact location.

She found out officially with a call from Scott's grandma. " I was by myself in our apartment," Jennifer said. I refused to believe it was his bank. I know it sounds weird because I was worried before I heard anything. When the news came, I was in denial." Her intuition had been right, and something was wrong. A family friend made the identification of Scott at the bank.

All three photos above of Jennifer and Scott, courtesy Jennifer Rios, 2019.

All three photos below are courtesy of Jennifer Rios, 2019

27

"It Ruined Father's Day for a Bunch of Us"

"FATHER'S DAY was never the same." Frank "Pancho," Redman said. Pancho knew Todd and Scott from Mission Trujillo, where he worked for sixteen years. He was a manager there. He nicknamed Todd, "Loco Oho," because of his crazy eyes. According to Frank, Scott, and Todd were both hard workers. He said that Scott was a bashful guy that didn't say much. Todd had an eye condition that rendered him legally blind. He had to have modifications to his driver's license to drive, according to Pancho.

The Friday night before the robbery, Todd came into Mission Trujillo very excited. Todd told Frank that he was excited because he had received a promotion at the bank. Todd said that he was no longer "Mastercard/Visa." He was now security. Pancho was concerned. "How are you going to use a gun with your eye problems, Todd?" He asked. Todd explained that this was the thing. The bank didn't use guns for security. Todd wouldn't have to carry a firearm. Pancho said, "No, guns? How are you going to protect all that money?" Pancho thought that the policy was "Total Bullshit." The following day, Todd was killed in the robbery.

"It still pisses me off." He said. I used to bank at the United Bank of Denver, but I moved all of my accounts after the robbery. They were so young." Pancho said. I have five children and twelve grandchildren, and I am never excited about Father's Day. "It's a very hard thing to talk about." Pancho's wife (Veronica) went to Metro with Todd. Todd was going to school to be a drug counselor. Scott wanted to be a police officer. Pancho has been at the Platte River Grill since 2000.

Pancho used to go fishing on the Green River (in both Colorado and Wyoming) with John Trujillo, and they sometimes took Todd. He thinks Scott may have come too. Pancho believes he has done that fishing trip about 75 times. Despite the twenty-year age gap, they were all friends. 'They had goals and direction in life. They were sweethearts, and they stuck together like glue." Pancho said. He said that he knew that Scott had fought back during the robbery. He agreed that there could very well be DNA on Scott's clothes or Bill McCullom's uniform. Of the robbery, Pancho believes it was a one-man job. He thinks it was either James King or Paul Yocum. He thinks Yocum may have been guilty of the 1990 robbery too. He stated that Yocum was no angel, and neither was James King.

Pancho always wanted to ask the foreperson of the jury what instructions (by the judge) made them acquit James King. The foreperson has told the media that the jury instructions forced them to acquit King. Joni Haack (the foreperson) has since passed away. Pancho believes that several of the jurors thought King was guilty. He did not attend the trial because he had to work. He did attend the joint funeral for Todd and Scott, where he heard Todd's father (John) speak. He wondered out loud if the case was even "open" anymore?

Pancho said *that this ruined Father's Day for a bunch of us. He says that on Father's Day, he always goes outside. Looks up to the sky and says, "Hi" to Scotty and Todd.*

28

"I got Todd the job at the bank."

"I got Todd the job at the bank as a clerk in the Mastercard/Visa Fraud Investigation Department." Thurston "Bird" Birdwell told me in a voice full of sadness and regret. "Todd was very good to work with." Bird said that Todd was a good kid. Bird believes the robbery was staged. He told the FBI this back in 1991 and 1992. He doesn't think that any money was actually taken and that the money was just moved to cover missing money in another department. Bird knew James King. According to Bird, King did it and that he had an accomplice.

According to Bird, he thinks he knows where the accomplice hid. He believes that the accomplice hid behind boxes in the file room where cigarette butts were found but never tested for DNA. There was evidence that someone had been hiding back there and smoking. As a member of the credit card fraud department and a close friend to the Wilson family, Bird was called to the scene the morning of the robbery. He was called while he was in church and told he needed to come down to the bank. He stated that he wasn't part of security, but the bank insisted that he come down to the scene anyway.

"The scene was very chaotic." He said. Bird was asked to identify the guards. He had known them all. He knew Todd and Scott personally and Phillip and Bill, from meetings at the bank. He knew why the supervisor's office door was kicked. "There was a video camera in there that the robber wanted to get to." He said. It turned out that the camera wasn't working that day. Some state that the camera had been moved to the guard shack, and the robber got the tape he wanted. Bird said that with the mantraps and the maze of tunnels, the robber had to be someone very familiar with the bank. "Had to be someone who really knew the place." He said.

In court, when the testimony was given regarding the tape from the supervisor's office, Bird stated that he heard James King tell Walter Gerash, " I'm home scott-free." Bird got very upset and was eventually asked to leave the courtroom. According to Bird, there was money missing from different departments, including from bank vice president, Bob Bardwell's department. That is why Bardwell's name was used in the robbery, "The bank was not secure." Bird said. Bird had told the police and FBI what he thinks, and they have told him to keep quiet. The president of the bank (at the time) told Bird not to say anything, but Bird said he would not be silenced. He lost his job of twelve years over it, but his conscience is clear.

"It's a complicated deal." He said. He thought maybe James King owed someone a favor. "I didn't care for him." Bird said of King. "I didn't trust him, and he wasn't an easy man to work with." He said. "King knew the maze."

Bird also stated that "things" floated around the security area, such as the fact that money had been stolen from the front counters before the robbery. Bird said that there was a lot going on there that people didn't know about before the robbery. "The bank was not a secure environment," he said. He didn't believe that James King had thrown his gun away.

According to Bird, the robbery was very traumatic. He had to come back to the Wilson house and tell John about Todd. John and DeLila were his best friends. "Grandma kept asking me if Todd was coming home, and I just shook my head, "No.," he said. He never understood the change in gun policy. Bird said that he carried a sidearm when he went out on fraud investigations. He was uncomfortable with Todd moving to security because of his sight problems, but Todd assured him that he would be fine. "Scott McCarthy was a tough guy." Bird said with a chuckle, but "Todd had never been a fight in his life."

Bird says that he sizes people up real quick, and he didn't like James King. He had an aura about him that I didn't trust. Bird saw King at the mall after the trial, and he just shook his head. "I actually thought about killing him myself, but I had a wife and a family to consider. " he said. Bird needed to think about his own life and family. His wife, Julie Chandler Birdwell, was a trust officer at the United Bank of Denver. Born in 1946, Bird is a military veteran. He was a United States Marine with three tours in Vietnam in 1966, 1967, and 1969.

Bird thinks DNA (with current techniques) is a good possibility. After the trial, the FBI told Bird to keep quiet because he couldn't prove anything. Because of his relationship with the Wilson family, he can't just sit back and say nothing. He has seen, firsthand, what this case has done to John and DeLila. They have no closure. Even though James King is dead, DNA testing could bring closure to the families. Bird would like to see the families get some answers and some closure. He would like to see justice.

29

"Look at my New Boots"

Thomas Tatalanski was the security section manager at the United Bank of Denver at the time of the robbery. He worked there for thirteen years. He left after the robbery because staying employed there was too painful for him. Tom took advantage of the counseling that the bank offered in the wake of the robbery and murders. He also reached out to the VA (as a former military person) to get counseling as well.

"I hired these guys," he said as I interviewed him on the phone one cold Denver day. He knew all four of them, and he was there to identify their bodies at the scene late on Father's Day of 1991. He remembered that it was challenging to be the middle manager. His boss would tell him what was to be done, and then he had to relay that to James Prado (the training supervisor) and the guards. He would hire and fire based on what his boss told him to do. All of the weekend guards were part-time, according to Tatalanski. They made minimum wage, and the benefits were not significant. There was some turnover among the weekend guards.

Before Norwest took over in April of 1991, he always offered new guards the opportunity to go and get licensed to carry a gun on the job. Tom didn't carry a weapon even though he had been in the military, "Not everyone should be carrying a gun," he said. After Norwest took over the bank, the policy changed, and the guards were unarmed. Tom was very emotional during our interview, and it wasn't very easy for him to discuss the trial and the slain guards. He remembered that the pressure of the trial was intense from all sides. There was pressure from the bank, the prosecution, and the defense.

During the trial, Tom's father was on his deathbed. He could not go to him because of his obligation to testify and how long he might be on the stand. He was also waiting behind James Prado in the line to testify, and Prado's testimony took longer than expected. Tatalanski would sit in the court hallway and wait to be called. His father died right after the trial, and Tom didn't get to see him before his death. He went to him afterward, which was the best he could do. It seemed as though that fact haunted him in the face of the fact that the jury acquitted James King. "I thought the jury got it," was all he could say. He would not discuss James King.

He remembered Bill McCullom as a funny man. "He didn't have a care in the world," he said. Tom remembered that on the Friday before the robbery, Todd Wilson has come in the guard room and put his feet up on the counter. "What do you think?' he asked Tom. "About what? Tom answered. "Look at my new boots," Todd said. After the murders, when Tom went to the scene, the first thing he noticed was those boots on Todd's feet. He said that it just broke him. "The Wilsons are such great people," he said.

Tom Tatalanski went to the funerals of the murdered guards. He has great difficulty speaking about the robbery and murders. In a light-hearted moment, he said that Gerash once mistook him for an FBI agent in the courtroom hallway because he was so well dressed for court.

30

R ule #1 is that You Go Home Every Night

Photo by Kimberli Roessing-Anderson, 2019

Photo by Kimberli
Roessing-Anderson, 2019

IT TOOK me a year to find James Prado, but he was well
worth the wait. After watching Prado testify on the VHS
tapes of the 1992 trial, I knew I had to try one more time to
find him. I made some calls and did some more research,
but it was a phone number from 1997 in Ancestry.com that
led me to him. I called and left a message, and the next day,
he called me back. He should be the last interview because
he is probably the one that knows the most about the security system, the guards, and the case. He is also the most
helpful guy. I interviewed him on the phone for over an
hour in December. We also met in person to talk further. He
was 34-years-old at the time of the robbery.

Jim Prado has now worked for the same company since
1992. He still works in security. United Bank fired him in
December of 1991 for having knowledge of security guards
eating in the monitor room. "They did me a favor, " he said.
Although it was upsetting that it happened right before
Christmas. He was called in from vacation on his daughter's
birthday. He returned home to his daughter's birthday party
and little girls running all over his house. He had to tell his
wife that he had been fired. Prado found a better position
with another company. He has been there for almost 28
years. He has been married for nearly 40 years. He has four
children. He is happy.

Prado remembers James King as very a very intelligent
man. He interviewed him first, and although he found a
spelling error on his resume, he liked King in the interview.
Prado stated that some cops are reactive in security jobs.
They only want to go out when something is happening. He

needed someone who would do the tours and be proactive in their approach. King was nothing if not proactive. "King was a "what if" kind of guy," he said. Changes were made at the bank based on some of James King's "what ifs." King once asked Prado what would happen in someone turned out the lights during a robbery. How would the cameras record? The bank started installing automatic security lights in their rooms with cameras.

King had been working for Maps Unlimited, but the work was giving him headaches, according to Prado. King was looking to do something that wouldn't strain his eyes. King was willing to do the tours and go beyond normal responsibilities. King liked the work. Prado taught king about the Mosler system, the Invisacom system, and gave him maps of the building. He thought King had worked at the bank for almost a year and that King carried his .38 Colt Trooper when he was on duty. King told Prado the reason he was working a second job was that he had been screwed-over on a house he had purchased. The foundation was cracked, and he didn't get the money out of it that he should have received. King told Prado that he and his wife had moved to a smaller house, and that was fine because it was just he and his wife now, and they didn't need a home that big.

Prado remembers that King had taken an unplanned vacation right before he resigned. He had an emergency in Mesa, Arizona, where his mother lived. Prado gave him the time and had his shift covered. Prado still had the request from King among his files. He also stated that when King resigned, it had been because Carol King was having health problems, and James King wanted to spend more time with her.

Prado didn't think that Paul Yocum had the smarts to rob

the bank in 1991. He described Paul Yocum as a hillbilly with a very successful father. Paul had been a disappointment to his father, according to Prado. Yocum had a string of menial jobs. Yocum's father was a prominent banker. Yocum loved his mother very much and had a good relationship with her. Prado also didn't believe that Yocum had robbed the bank in 1990 for which he was acquitted.

Prado stated that Mike McKown was also a suspect in the 1991 robbery. He was initially the main suspect. He was in Kent, Washington (near Seattle), staying with his sister. The FBI went there to interview them both. McKown claimed to have been in Kent when the robbery happened, and his family alibied him. He had been in Denver two weeks earlier and met up with James King, according to Prado. After the trial, McKown called Prado and told him that he had suffered a stroke a couple of days after he testified. The last Prado had heard, McKown was working for King Soopers as a driver. I was able not been able to reach Mike McKown for an interview.

Prado explained that one of the issues with the security at United Bank of Denver and then Norwest was that the "big shots" who worked in building one would often forget their security passes on the weekends. This was before lanyards were popular, and employees carried the cards in their wallets or pockets. Employees would call from the security phone and want a guard to come and let them into the building. If a guard refused or gave them grief, Tom Tatalanski or Alvin Lutz would get a phone call on Monday. They big shots expected the security guards to know their names and faces. At the time of the robbery, there were seventy-eight vice presidents. A book was sent up to the monitor room with pictures and names. Guards could also utilize the computer to identify employees. Still, the guards were told that even if they could not locate the person, they were to go and escort them into the bank anyway.

Prado was at church with his family on Father's Day, 1991. He had gone to bed early the night before because Father's Day and Mother's Day were popular days for guards to call in sick. He was pleasantly surprised when that didn't happen the following morning. Little did he know what awaited him when he returned from church. He had a message from Danell Taylor but as soon as he came into the house his phone rang again. "Get your ass down here; we have just been robbed," said Bev Bennett from the bank. Prado dressed in his uniform and headed for the bank.

When Prado arrived at the scene. He identified the bodies and took it all in. He had a person in mind immediately. I won't name that person here, but Jim Prado felt he knew who could do this sort of thing. He thought there were two people. He felt as though one person committed the killing, and another (possibly King) did the robbery. Prado also thought it was incredibly dangerous for the shooter to have shot Mankoff and McCarthy in the battery room. He said if one of the rounds had struck one of the batteries, they would have exploded. Prado also thought it ironic that right beside the monitor room where three of the guards lay dead was a locked locker with twenty-two revolvers inside.

Jim Prado said that the feeling of seeing the four guards lying dead was surreal. "I didn't believe it," he said. There were dread and fear. He had just spoken with all four of these men in the previous two days. He had joked and laughed with them. "There was blood everywhere," Prado said. He remembered how Scott McCarthy was draped over Phil Mankoff. Weeks later, Tom Tatalaski asked Jim to pull the uniforms of the dead guards from the closet. Scott McCarthy didn't have a uniform yet, but he was able to pull the other three. When he looked at the white shirts, he could visualize the blood and the bullet holes. He saw the shirts still soaked in blood.

Following the robbery, Prado stated that the Denver Police Department babysat the guards for a long time. The bank also hired outside contractors to help. "It was turmoil," he said. Prado was trying to train eight new guards and get them ready. Guards had quit, and some had been fired. Some had been suspended. The bank had clamped down hard on the rules. By the end of September, Prado found himself out of a job too. The man who knew the most about the security system and had been with the company for fifteen years was fired for a missing gap in a security tape where two guards were eating in the monitor room.

Prado talked about the conversation he had with Scott McCarthy the night before the robbery. "Scott called me and wanted to come in and get started. I explained to him that I didn't have the hire approved yet, but sometimes a person can start and get paid retroactively." That is what Scott wanted to do. Tom Tatalanski ok'd it. In hindsight, he wished he hadn't. He also had a conversation with Todd Wilson a few days before that haunts him. On the Thursday before the robbery, Wilson (who had only moved to the security department a few days before) was walking a tour with Prado when he stopped on a bridge and asked, "What do I do if things ever get physical," he asked? "Am I allowed to defend myself?" Todd had encountered a homeless man a few nights before hiding in a bathroom. The man didn't want to leave. Prado said that Todd was just a little nervous. " Homeless people hiding in the bank were not a high priority for the Denver Police Department," Prado said.

Prado told him, the most important thing is that you go home every night. You defend yourself; however, you can.

Use your flashlight. Anything is game." That conversation bothers Jim Prado because two days later, he was standing over Todd's body. Prado thinks that Wilson was unable to find the alarm in Stairwell C and had come back to get help from Phil Mankoff. As he entered the monitor room, he found it empty and walked back to the battery room where the robber ambushed him. Prado thinks this is how Wilson ended up being shot from the back.

Prado believes that King had the intelligence and the knowledge to have participated in the robbery. After the verdict, he thought several things: There goes his life (meaning King). Maybe they arrested the wrong guy? This is never going to be over. Jim Prado believes that the robber expected two guards to be there on Father's Day. Sundays were usually two-guard days, and rarely did they have enough staff to have a swing guard. He thinks that one man did the killing, and the other man did the robbing. Even though the police and FBI raised the print from the log sheet (what he calls a Perry Mason moment), there was nothing unusual on it. It was Mankoff's writing, and the last entry was Wilson being dispatched to the stairwell alarm.

Of Bill McCullom, Prado said he was a very quiet guy. He explained that McCullom lived with his mom, and all he talked about what getting out on his own. "He wanted to get his own place and get his own car, " he said. Prado stated that it was sometimes awkward to go on a tour with McCullom because he didn't talk much. He noted that McCullom was always mature in his work ethic. He was always contentious about his job duties.

Of Phil Mankoff, Prado said he had a great sense of humor and was fun to work with on tour. Phil talked about his step-daughter all the time. "He wanted to get her this and get her that," Prado said. "He really loved that little girl."

Twice divorced, Phil was less happy with women in general. "He was a little bitter toward women-his exes," he said. Mankoff would tell Prado that he had other irons in the fire, and he could leave with only two-days-notice.

Some of the other things Prado thought about the robbery were that the robber/murderer left the tape by accident, or he ran out of room in his bag for it. He believed that the robber may have been trying to get into the supervisor's office because the fingerprint cards were kept in there. About the records tunnel, Prado said that the Trust-Vault records were held there. Prado thought someone could have been hiding in that room before the robbery. Behind some files, boxes were 30-40 cigarette butts and a disposable coffee cup. It wasn't a cup from the bank's cafeteria. Prado also noted that the bank soda machines did not carry 7up as a product. There was a 7up can found at the scene.

After the robbery, Prado brought these issues to the attention of a police officer, Sue Scott (who was helping in the investigation). She put them in plastic bags and had them booked into evidence. No one knows if all of these items have been tested for prints or DNA. Scott told Prado that Jon Priest jumped all over her for collecting that evidence. Priest informed Scott that this was his investigation, and everything had to go through him first. Scott wanted to know if she should have called him in the middle of the night because she found cigarette butts and a coffee cup? This evidence did not fit the prosecution narrative that one person came in and did the robbery and the killing. This evidence indicated that someone may have been hiding in that room. One local newspaper reported that there was a "butt print" in the dust and dirt where someone had been sitting there on the floor.

Prado indicated that Sue Scott (DPD) put the cigarette

butts and the coffee cup into evidence. She also researched where the cup (which had a bird logo on it) could have come from, and she called Nobel/Cisco. She discovered that the only business in the area that ordered those cups was the Marriott Hotel. They had those cups in their lobby. Since United Bank didn't carry 7up products, Sue Scott also tried to figure out who sold 7up nearby. The cigarettes were in a pile on the floor. Any or all of these items could have DNA on them. Have they been tested?

The final thoughts from Prado are that he is not bitter with the bank. He is happy where he is working and has good benefits and pay. He believes there is enough evidence out there to secure a conviction of someone. Someone needs to put it all together and find the person or persons that did this. If it was James King, then prove it was James King. Prado believes DNA could be used in this process on items such as William McCullom's uniform and Scott McCarthy's clothes. He wonders if they cigarette butts and the coffee cup that he found were ever tested? Prado says that every once in a while, a cold-case detective from DPD contacts him, but nothing comes from it. They all want him to take them on a tour of the bank, and the bank won't allow it.

The duties of a weekend guard at the United Bank of Denver were different than the full-time guards that worked Monday through Friday. Weekend guards were guarding a bank that was closed. They went on tours of specific areas and checked to make sure doors were locked. They used their Markey cards to check-in at Detex stations. They would turn their key in the Detex box to show that they were compliant on their security tours. They were there in case something went wrong. They toured floors 1-13 and the below-ground levels floors. They also were in charge of floors 51 and 52. United Bank of Denver One of UBCI was the administration building. These were the offices. United Bank of Denver, Two of UBC2, was the facilities building and the building with the atrium. United Bank of Denver Three or UBC3 was the building with vaults and security.

Prado explained that the bank went through a few different uniforms while he worked there. At one point, they wore brown uniforms. He said there was a change to white shirts, gray pants, and black shoes. This is the uniform that was worn when the 1991 robbery happened. After Norwest took over and the guns were taken away, they added a Navy-blue sports jacket. Norwest wanted a more formal look. Possibly a sports jacket hides the fact that a guard is not carrying a gun. When a guard started, they would wear what was available in terms of used uniforms until their uniform was ordered.

Prado also explained the parking garage. There was a lot of testimony about the garage and where employees were supposed to park and the arm of the parking garage being in the up position on the day of the robbery. Prado doesn't know why the arm was in the up position on the day of the robbery. It should not have been. Employees generally parked on the 3rd floor because the entrance to the bridge was on the third floor. They didn't advertise that fact because the third floor was supposed to be for customer parking. The bank charged employees to park, so employees had to have a parking pass. Customers were issued tickets that could be validated in the bank. Some employees parked on side streets to avoid having to pay to park.

The 7th-floor parking was where the United Bank of Denver kept its fleet of vehicles, and there was a car wash on that floor for bank vehicles. Some employees parked on the 7th floor. Witnesses at trial stated that Paul Yocum always parked on the 7th floor. At trial, there was testimony that a

pair of disposable gloves and other items were found in a
trash can on the 7th floor of the parking garage. These items
were collected and tested for fingerprints, hair, and fibers
(Denver County, 1992).

James Prado explained that working at the United Bank
of Denver, the robbery, and the trial made him a wiser man.
He writes down names, dates, and times. He keeps a journal
of sorts. Prado keeps notes. "You are not going to remember
where you were two weeks ago and who you talked with
unless you write it down," he said. He has also tried to learn
not to smile when he is nervous. He smiled a lot while he
was testifying, and the prosecutor was not happy with him.
During a break in court, Bill Buckley chastised him for
smiling too much. He also smiled when he was identifying
James King. "Stop smiling!" Buckley told him during the
break. I found that James Prado still smiles a lot, and I think
that is a good thing. Below notes from a conversation James
Prado had with Mike McKown after the trial:

Mike McKown
Teaching school
following day
Contacted Seattle FBI
King Mailed latter Seattle
took wife to work then
went to Chess Club closed
No Alibi
Took shoes
Checked his storage shed
operation Phoenix CIA
Disassembled his car
at Fire station
Shares house with Sister
Graduation in June - Niece
Daughters arrive 10:27 Imnotsuite.
King Cut his own keys
During Divorce McKown lost his .357
8 months ago
2 days after Trial Stroke

PART V

NEXT?

31

F orensics
        I could start this chapter with the words: "Not
        Much," but that would be a disservice to the
evidence that was collected, the people that collected it, and
what is available now for re-testing. As I have stated repeat-
edly, DNA testing was in its infancy in 1992. From court testimony, it appears that blood was tested to see if it was indeed
blood, animal or human, and for blood type. In 2019, DNA
was thriving, and a re-examination of guard uniforms and
Scott McCarthy's clothes could help move this case forward.
All aspects of forensic testing have progressed since 1991. All
of the evidence should be re-tested.

Only .38 bullets were used in the murders, and we know
they were fired from a Colt Trooper. There were six lands
and grooves with a left twist. Eighteen rounds were fired.
Seventeen went into the guards, and one went into the door
of the supervisor's office. None of the fragments at the scene
were of value. Some of the bullets were hollow points.
Ammunition came from three manufacturers: Winchester,
Federal, and Remington. The bullets that entered McCul-

lom's body had a ring shape on the bottom. None of the guards had powder burns on their shirts, meaning that the maximum distance had been exceeded. No one clarified at trial what the maximum distance is for powder burns.

Six usable fingerprints were found at the scene, yet only eleven print cards were tested. Why only eleven? I would think the investigators would want to test every former guard that was a suspect. They had at least 50 suspects. To be an FBI match, 10 points must match in the fingerprint. Two footprints were found at the scene. One was in the incinerator room near Bill McCullom's body. The other print was found on the glass outside the security supervisor's office. There was a Grandma's Cookie Bag in the monitor room that had Scott McCarthy's fingerprint. In the trash can on the 7th floor of the parking garage, the following items were found: Pepsi cup, plastic bag (palm print), plastic cardholder (print), cigarette pack, single-use plastic gloves, Diet-Pepsi cardboard carrier (two prints). The gloves were mailed to the FBI for further testing. Could the prints be run through fingerprint databases now?

None of the items other than the cookie bag had the victim's prints. None had prints from James King. There was a palm print inside the battery room. There was an unusable print from a VCR in the monitor room. The Mt. Dew can had a print from a guard, Harry Glass. The 7up can and coffee cup in the file room had no usable prints. Harry Glass had also purchased shoes similar to those that made the footprint on the glass of the supervisor's office. That print was similar to the one found in the dirt by William McCullom's body. The shoes bought by Glass (Stacy Adams) were a different size and color.

Single-use latex gloves were found in the trash bin on the seventh floor of the parking garage. The gloves were absent of hair or fiber. The gloves were dirty and thin. The single-use gloves come in boxes of one-hundred. Yankee 91 also used these type gloves at the scene.

At the scene, a Mt. Dew can was found propping open a door in the monitor room. A former employee, Doug Bagley, had been fired for propping open the door in the monitor room. A 7up can was found in the records tunnel. There were cigarette butts and a coffee cup found in the file room (located behind the monitor room) and another cigarette butt in the records tunnel. Have these items been tested for DNA? Several of the guards testified at trial that there would have been no reason for someone to sit on the floor behind file boxes and smoke in the file room. There were lounges to eat, drink, and smoke that were available. There were couches if someone wanted to take a nap.

32

I s the Case still Open?

UPON FILING various FOIAs (Freedom of Information Act)
with the Denver Police, I was told that the case is still open.
They denied me access to any of the police files. They would
not be interviewed. I was only able to get a mugshot because
those are public records. I asked them when the last time
they worked on the case was, and they would not answer
that question either. I don't think they are working the case.
I know the FBI offered a 100k reward after the trial for new
information, but the case seems pretty cold. If investigators
feel the same way as Bill Buckley feels, the man who
committed the crime was acquitted and is now deceased. I
am not sure the DPD will ever look for another suspect of
their own accord.

I wonder if they still have the clothes and uniforms
of the guards, could new more advanced DNA testing be

attempted? Since we know that the robber dragged William McCullom to another room, could there be touch DNA present or DNA from sweat? Was the robber sweating while he was dragging another full-grown man to another room? If Scott McCarthy attempted to fight back, could there be touch DNA on him? The robber could have touched any of the slain guards when he was taking their radios, keys, or pass cards. He may have left some DNA on any of these items. It could be DNA that was not able to be tested in 1991-1992. **Yet, nothing will happen if these items sit boxed on an evidence shelf somewhere untested.**

There is a lab near Reston, Virginia, called Parabon Nanolabs, which has been featured on several "Dateline" episodes. Parabon NanoLabs, a subsidiary of Parabon Computation, was founded in 2008 by Steven Armentrout, Michael Norton, and Christopher Dwyer.

Snapshot DNA Phenotyping Service is the name of a DNA phenotyping tool developed by Parabon NanoLabs, which creates composite face imaging sketches based on DNA samples. In cooperation with American law enforcement, Parabon uploaded DNA evidence from crime scenes to GEDmatch in an attempt to identify perpetrators (Wikipedia, 2019).

In November 2018, Parabon said they were working on 200 cases, 55% had produced leads, and in May 2019, they said they were solving cold cases at the rate of one a week (Wikipedia, 2019). Having watched the "Dateline" episodes where Parabon was featured, the likeness to the suspects in testing was unbelievable. Once the profile is complete, it can then be aged similar to what is done with missing children at the Center for Missing and Exploited Children by artists who specialize in aging portraits. The cost is about

$4000.00 a profile (Wikipedia, 2019). The current turn-around time is about 45 days (Wikipedia, 2019).

DNA phenotyping is the process of predicting an organism's phenotype using only genetic information collected from genotyping or DNA sequencing. This term, also known as molecular photo fitting, is primarily used to refer to the prediction of a person's physical appearance and/or biogeographic ancestry for forensic purposes. DNA phenotyping uses many of the same scientific methods as those being used for genetically-informed personalized medicine, in which drug responsiveness (pharmacoge-nomics) and medical outcomes are predicted from a patient's genetic information. Significant genetic variants associated with a particular trait are discovered using a genome-wide association study (GWAS) approach, in which hundreds of thousands or millions of single-nucleotide polymorphisms (SNPs) are tested for their association with each trait of interest. Predictive modeling is then used to build a mathematical model for making trait predictions about new subjects (Wikipedia, 2019).

If James King was guilty, the DNA could tell that story. If he was not guilty, the DNA may tell that story and give the police a new suspect to investigate. There is no downside. There are fingerprints, footprints, and fiber evidence in the case. How long has it been since that evidence has been re-tested? How has that testing changed and improved in 28 years? I think there could be a resolution to this case in the science. The science may not have been available in 1991 or 1992, but it could be there now. Cases are being solved by putting DNA samples into Ancestry.com. Parabon is solving cold cases every day.

An acquittal doesn't have to mean the end of an investigation. A jury stated unanimously that there wasn't enough evidence to convict James King. Take their doubts and answer them. They doubted it was just one person. They didn't understand why the robber didn't smell of smoke after firing eighteen shots at the guards. Some of the jurors were unsure of the identification process. The jurors wanted to see more direct evidence. Science could answer these questions.

EXAMPLE from the Parabon
   Nano-labs website, 2019

33

L ike a Blood Diamond

LIKE A BLOOD DIAMOND that keeps dripping, so do the dollars from the robbery. Unmarked, the money will never be found if spent in low amounts on mundane items. Give a cashier a fifty-dollar bill for some things at a grocery store and get back thirty new, untainted dollars in change. Clean the money. Launder it. Pay for your gasoline in cash. Pay for a pizza in cash. Tip with cash. Two-hundred thousand dollars could last a long time if spent in small amounts in everyday places. We all have that one friend who always has cash and pays in cash.

The cash isn't the tricky part. It's the blood. How do you wash that blood from your hands? The guards were such young men. Twenty-one is so young. Two of these young men still had one foot in their high school yearbooks. They were going to be husbands and fathers. They had parents and siblings. They had lives. In an instant, they were gone, and sinkholes appeared in the lives of their families and friends. I wonder what the robber thought when he saw their ages (later on television) as I am sure he was watching.

Perched in an armchair or a recliner looking at his work, what did he think? Did he have kids that age? Thirty-three and forty-one are the ages of young men too. They had lives as well. These men had families and a purpose. I often wonder if his palms were sweaty and did his heartbeat increase when their pictures and stories came on TV. Did he become uncomfortable and change positions? Was he agitated? This is blood one can never wash off oneself. Every time he saw a young man who resembled one of the guards, did he see their faces? I bet he did.

It would be sad to think that four men died for mundane items like toothpaste, gasoline, or pizza. Did the robber every buy anything substantial with the money from the robbery? He would be careful not to draw attention to himself by making a large purchase. Was there satisfaction just in getting away with the robbery and not being caught? Is the money in someone's attic in a black doctor's bag, unspent? Was the robber too afraid to ever use any of it for fear of getting caught? Did the color rise in his face whenever he thought about the robbery or watched coverage of the case on television? Did he jump when the phone rang?

If one is religious, what will they say at the gate to Heaven when one has killed four young men for money? How is that explained? Fragility and disease can make for a sympathetic figure at the end of one's life. Wrinkles and age spots replace smooth, spotless skin. Hair falls out or turns gray. Older people move more slowly. They may not see or hear as well as they used to, and people yield to them in ways they only do for older folks. However, when one looks in the mirror, do they still see that man in his fifties wearing a fedora and mirrored sunglasses? Do they see the tweed dress jacket? Can they hear the gunfire, and are their hands still stained with blood? Paraphrasing Bill Buckley, he (the robber) couldn't dig the bullets out of the bodies and take them with him. That is true. He also couldn't know how the science of DNA would explode in the years after the robbery. There is evidence in this case; it just has to be worked.

Are you that one person they told? Are you the person they confided in because they either had to tell someone out of guilt or they had to tell someone out of glory? Why are you still silent? So many people would be relieved to know the truth, and you could provide that relief. You would be forgiven. Hearing a confession is not a crime. Keeping someone's secret is not a crime. Staying silent is a horrible burden. Would you not like some relief too?

This crime may not ever be solved. The DPD and the District Attorney's Office feel as though they had the right man, and he was acquitted in a court of law. While writing this book, there have been days that I was sure James King was guilty, and there have been days I knew he was innocent. I look at the life of James King, and I don't see why he would do such a horrendous thing when he had sons of his own that were roughly the same age as the guards. I am also of the opinion that this may have been more than one person. How could a man kill four people (three at close range) and have no blood splatter on him when he arrived at the vault? How could he not smell of something?

On the other hand, I didn't know Jim King. I only know him through his sister and brother. I remember him through old black and white pictures and stories told by

people who loved him. Those people believe he was innocent. I will say that there was a damning circumstantial case
against him. At around the same time of the robbery, King
shaved his mustache, lost his driver's license, threw away his
gun, upgraded his bank box, had a shaky alibi, was a former
DPD police officer who had access to mixed ammunition,
and happened to be a retired United Bank of Denver security guard. He knew the security system and had maps of the
bank as all the security guards did. He looked like the
sketch. Although I will say that it was not hard to make the
former guards look like the sketch. Once you stick a fedora,
mirrored sunglasses, and a mustache on a middle-aged
man, he starts to resemble the sketch.

Today, this crime would have been solved. There are
street camera's everywhere. Some neighbor's RING would
have caught the robber leaving or coming home from the
bank. DNA would have been found and tested. Google
Home, or Alexa, would have heard a discussion. Social
media and browsing history would have been tracked.
Traffic cameras would have seen the car. Cell towers would
have followed his cell phone or even his vehicle's navigation
system. 'Dateline NBC' would have video of him buying his
disguise or burner phone at Walmart. Ballistics and forensic
evidence analysis has improved. This case would have been
solved. In 1991, we still relied heavily on eye-witness testimony and circumstantial evidence because that is what was
available. The DNA testing was in its infancy.

I would also make the observation that I doubt this
robber went out and bought his disguise. I believe he used
things he already had at home or found tucked away in storage. He wore dated clothes and mirrored sunglasses. The
shoes could have come from anywhere. Some criminals will
wear a shoe that doesn't fit during the crime to try and

throw off the police at the scene. I was behind a man at
Walmart one day when he placed a shovel, tarp, gloves and
duct tape on the conveyer belt that takes those items down
to the cashier. He looked at me, and I looked at him. *Not a
smart man.* This may have been an innocent purchase, but it
looked terrible. I wanted to say, "See you on, Dateline!"

For the families of the guards and the six other
victims, in this case, I would like to see it solved. A further
DNA analysis of the clothes worn by the guards might yield
clues. Is there an item in evidence that we know the robber
touched with his bare hands? The vault tellers stated that he
was not wearing gloves. The only answers left for this
robbery are held in forensic evidence or a confession. Did
the robber tell someone, or is he still alive and willing to
admit his guilt? I am not betting on a confession, but there
might be someone who knows the truth that has not come
forward. Pressure should be put on the DPD and the
District Attorney's Office to open the case for review and
further DNA analysis. In an age where law enforcement is
closing cold cases by putting DNA profiles into Ancestry.-
com, I am confident there are some options out there to
close this case.

*James W. King died on May 21, 2013, at St. Johns in
Lakewood, Colorado. He had been ill with dementia for
many years. He was 77-years-old.

34

Author's Thoughts

A Trip Downtown

My husband and I went downtown to find the memorial to the guards first in June of 2019. We were carrying our big bulky cameras and camera bags. We had our cell phones, which sometimes take better pictures. It was hot, and the air was thick. It was a partly cloudy day, which is not the norm for Denver. I could feel some humidity in the air. We could not go far as our two Boston Bull Terriers were in the car. Even with air conditioning, water, and Puppiccinos from Starbucks, they sound as if they are being ax-murdered if we are out of their sight. We found the right spot in the back of the cash register building and began looking.

There was a lot of over-growth and foliage. We walked under trees and through weeds, and we couldn't find it. I was using a picture from a book and an image from a People Magazine article to guide me. It was a Sunday. The area is filled with benches and tables with chairs. I am sure it hops on weekdays, but that day it was dead. I have never liked that building because the robbery and murders are the first things I think of when I see it on the skyline. It wasn't any better close up. It was stale, and spaces, where people smoke cigarettes on the breaks, carried that scent. Although there were plenty of places to discard cigarette butts, butts still littered the ground.

We moved tall grass and bushes. We bent under tree branches. We could not find the memorial. We wondered if the bank had removed it for some reason. We eventually gave up and drove the King house in Golden, Colorado. It took a lot longer than 10 minutes. I had old pictures of the house, but it has been 28 years, so we used navigation. The house is smaller in person than it looks in pictures. It had been recently sold, and a new driveway had been poured. Contractors were painting and working on the house. Some doors were open, and I was able to peek around. I remembered how Jim's brother (Tom) had commented on how small the house on Juniper was compared with the house King had owned before the bankruptcy. Tom stated that his brother had owned a large two-story home in Westminster.

The Juniper house is listed on Zillow as having four bedrooms, but they must be small. The shrubs and other bushes were gone. The prominent tree in the 1991 photos chopped down. The house sat all alone. A large garage sat behind it. If those walls in the Juniper house could speak? We took some pictures and left. The house looked as if it had not seen love in a while. Greg King was the last owner before the latest sale. There is no landscaping, just a house on some grass. The house is a bluish-gray color with a white awning. Somehow, a couple of rose bushes in front of the house have survived and were in bloom. It was a sad-looking little house.

In October, we went back to the bank building with

renewed hope of finding the memorial for the guards. We had studied the photos closer and realized that the monument was on a small incline. Brian thought he knew where it might be, and he was right. After a lengthy conversation with two people who were on drugs and a homeless person sleeping on a bench nearby, Brian found it. It is small. I don't say that with any disrespect. It states that it was paid for by employees, and that may have been all the money they had available to them. I would have thought that the bank (itself) would have constructed something more profound for the four men who lost their lives doing their job. We took pictures and left. I was troubled by the site of it. I felt as though it was a metaphor for the entire situation. The effort was too small and even more difficult to find.

It might be up to the public to help solve this case. Pressure from the public and the media might persuade the DPD and the FBI to solve this case. The investigators would have to put some money and resources into it. They would have to be willing to start over. DNA and fingerprints testing is costly. As a reader and interested party in this story, what can you do? Call the DPD and the FBI and ask about the case. Call The Denver Post and the local news channels and ask about the case. As taxpayers, the government agencies answer to you. The media can help apply some pressure if there is a public interest in the case. The reader will have to take the case from here. Make some calls and ask some questions. I will keep the website at www.Frigid-averycoldcase.com updated. We also a page on Facebook and Instagram.

PHOTO of the memorial and Juniper house
    Taken by Kimberli Roessing-Anderson, 2019

THE CONTENTS of the James W. King Safety Deposit Box
    Wills for James W. King and his mother, Doris Louise
Keplinger Ette King
    Baptism certificates
    Birth Certificates for: Carol, James, David, Gregory, and
James King Jr.

Marriage License for James and Carol King

Deed for the Juniper house, payment book for mortgage

Military records for James King and his son, Gregory King

Life insurance policy from State Farm

Passports

Denver Police Department retirement card

1980 Ford Fiesta car title

Tax records prior to 1991

Files on personal property

Check registers/cancelled checks

Computer disks

Jewelry and appliance information/warranties

Rough drafts of King's writings

Not in the box: *car deeds from David King's multiple cars (this was one of the reasons King was upgrading to a larger box).*

The money from the robbery

TERMS AND FACTS TO **Remember**

A LIFE WHAT FOR? – the non-fiction piece James King was writing when he was arrested.

BLUE GUARD BOOK-FORMER United Bank of Denver guards

BUCKET OF AMMO-POLICE officers change manufactures of ammunition frequently and discarded ammunition is collected in buckets that are kept at the DPD contracted firing range or at officer's houses. This ammunition is referred to as **Mixed Ammunition**. Officers sometimes have mixed ammunition from different manufacturers in their firearms.

CODES FOR SECURITY Keys-keys set up to match your job description are called **Markey** cards. There were codes for master keys for example : **UBC1MK1**-stands for United Bank Center One Master Key1-this would key would open all sections.

DETEX BOXES and **Detex Stations**-Security guards would stop and the stations and turn their key in the box to show that they had been completing their security tours. These stations were spread out along their security routes.

DPD-DENVER POLICE DEPARTMENT

INVISACOM-THE PART of the security system that dealt with time zones. A certain part of the bank could be sectioned off if no one was supposed to be in there (for example on a Sunday) and if someone went into that area; an alarm would go off.

JULY 3RD-5TH PHOTO **Line-up**-this is the line-up shown to the six vault tellers that led to James King's arrest. It was considered by some to be tainted because King's photo was the only photo that was also in the blue guard book shown to the tellers on June 20th for five of the vault tellers and the

26th for Nine McGinty. You will also hear about line-ups such as: the Yocum line-up and the McKown line-up. These are line-ups for particular past guards.

MANTRAP-A SMALL ROOM with a door on each side and window glass. If one door is opened before the other is closed; the occupant is trapped. If the occupant doesn't have the correct credentials encoded to his or her security pass; they are trapped. This was part of the security system at the United Bank of Denver in 1991.

MARKEY CARD- THIS WAS a security card that bank employees had to carry

MOSLER SYSTEM-A SECURITY SYSTEM installed at the United Bank of Denver that dispenses tape like a receipt to show what alarms have been activated. System connected to the alarms

MOTION IN LIMINE-MOTIONS made outside the presence of the jury.

POLICE PROCEDURE MANUAL-JAMES KING was writing one before the trial

RED GUARD BOOK-CURRENT United Bank of Denver guards

. . .

RELOADER-A PERSON THAT LOADS their own ammunition with powder and will sometimes have a reloading table they work from with their equipment.

UNITED BANK OF DENVER was purchased by **Norwest Bank** in 1991. Norwest changed the gun policy. In 1998, Norwest and **Wells Fargo** merged.

VOICE DIRE-THE EXAMINATION of a juror or witness by the judge or counsel.

WOODWARD INTERVIEW- PAULA WOODWARD interviewed **Paul Yocum** for 9 News before the trial. Many of the jurors admitted to watching the interview.

YANKEE 91- A CODE name for the Denver Crime Lab

302 REPORT-AN FBI REPORT filed when they conduct an interview

+P+ Ammunition-a type of ammunition that was used in the robbery and murders that law enforcement use only.

THE VHS TAPES

The VHS Tapes Taken by the Robber
    Tape #1 Atrium Tape
    Tape #2 Main Lobby
    Tape #3 North Vestibule
    Tape #5 Armored Car Parking Garage
    Tape #6 Cash Vault
    Tape #7 Parking Lot
    Tape #8 Cash Vault
    Tape #9 Motor Bank One Loading Dock
    Tape #10 Night Depository on Broadway
    Tape #11 South Vestibule

Tape #4 Was left behind. This camera focused on 17th and Grant. The recording was of guard, William McCullom, at around 2:30 a.m. on his tour at 17th and Grant. No one knows why the robber/murderer left that tape. Was it a clue? Did he run out room in his bag? Did he miss it?

*The camera that would have shown the robber at the security phone was fuzzy, distorted and unable to provide a clear picture. This was known to security and a new camera had been

requested to replace it. It had not arrived by the day of the robbery.

The camera in the freight elevator was a dummy camera. What happened once William McCullom let the robber inside the elevator is unknown.

DISTRICT COURT, CITY AND COUNTY OF DENVER, COLORADO

Case No. 91CR2466, Courtroom 11

AFFIDAVIT OF INSOLVENCY

PEOPLE OF THE STATE OF COLORADO,

Plaintiff,

vs.

JAMES W. KING,

Defendant.

STATE OF COLORADO   }
                    } ss.
City and County of Denver)

JAMES W. KING, being sworn, deposes and states:

1. That he is insolvent and has no funds with which to pay investigatory costs and attorney fees in the above-entitled matter.

2. That he is currently incarcerated, and his family receives a monthly pension in the amount of $1,739.00.

3. That the monthly family expenses are as follows:

House payment	$ 684.00
Public Service	94.00
Telephone	36.97
Water and sewer	41.00
Cable	41.05
Newspaper	9.20
Medical insurance	344.14
Car insurance	26.93
Life insurance	30.00
Trash removal	12.45
Charge accounts	147.00
Rx medicines	34.96
Car, gasoline	40.00
Eyeglasses	92.00
Attorney fees, payment	200.00
Total	$1,825.31

4. My wife, Carolyn King, is paid $500/mo., which amount is used for groceries, dog food, and miscellaneous items.

Further affiant saith naught.

James W. King

Subscribed and sworn to before me this 19 day of March, 1992.

Courtesy, Denver County, 2019

Defense shifts focus away from King in United Bank killings

Rental car agents testify

Associated Press

DENVER — Lawyers began presenting their defense for James King on Tuesday with testimony from rental car agents who may have seen the man who killed four guards in the Father's Day 1991 robbery of United Bank.

Walter Gerash and Scott Robinson began questioning five rental car employees at Stapleton International Airport, where, soon after the bank was robbed of nearly $198,000, a man who said he was traveling to Los Angeles sought to lease a rental car for cash.

Lloyd Quintana, airport service representative, said he saw the man, who appeared bewildered and lost, at the airport's baggage area. "He said he wanted to rent a car, and that he had $100,000 on him," Quintana said.

He said the man carried a brown "doctor bag" that appeared heavy, and that he appeared to be from 50 to 55 years old, with "grayish salt-and-pepper hair," with a moustache that was "kinda gray." He was about 6 feet tall with a small white scar on the left side of his face.

Workers at the bank said the man who robbed them had a moustache but wore a hat. He appeared to have gray hair and wore a Band-Aid on the side of his face.

Other witnesses, who worked at rental car agencies, gave varying physical descriptions of the man they talked to but confirmed he had asked them about renting cars and said he would pay in cash.

Gerash and Robinson then began probing police and FBI investigations of Paul Yocum, a former bank guard who was questioned about the June 16 robbery.

Police viewed Yocum as a possible suspect because he had been accused and acquitted of the May 26, 1990, theft of $29,000 from a United Bank automated teller machine.

Authorities said some of the .38-caliber ammunition seized in a search of Yocum's apartment in Denver and his mother's home in Flagler was consistent with the type used in the United Bank slayings, but forensic analysis showed the bullets that killed the four guards were fired from a .38-caliber Colt revolver similar to the type once carried by King's pistol, not Yocum's.

King: Defense lawyers begin their case.

Gazette Telegraph

Courtesy, Gazette Telegraph, 1992

UNITED BANK GUARDS' TIMELINE

Here is a schedule showing partial movements of the four bank guards killed in the June 16 robbery at the United Bank of Denver.

It is based on security monitoring records, but does not reflect every guard activity. No videotapes or guard log sheets were found at the bank to help fill in the gaps.

12:40 a.m.: Guards Philip Mankoff and William McCullom Jr. were in the monitoring room.

12:42 a.m.: Alarm sounds at the north vestibule.

12:46 a.m.: Mankoff responds to alarm. Records show he did not re-enter the monitoring room using his access card until 6:43 a.m. But bank officials said it was possible McCullom buzzed him back into the room, which would not be reflected in the security records.

12:50 a.m.: McCullom leaves the monitoring room to make rounds of the United Bank Center.

2:26 a.m.: McCullom exits and re-enters the bank at the Sherman Street door, which was not a part of the regular rounds.

3:54 a.m.: McCullom enters the cash vault.

4 a.m.: McCullom enters the monitoring room.

3:06 a.m.: Alarm sounds in a records tunnel near the cash vault.

5:04 a.m.: Security system automatically resets alarm.

5:04 a.m.: Guard in monitoring room turns the record tunnel alarm off. The alarm is not reactivated until 9:33 a.m., after the

time which authorities believe the guards were killed.

7:54 a.m.: Mankoff and trainee guard Scott McCarthy enter the cash vault.

7:59 a.m.: Mankoff and McCarthy exit cash vault.

8 a.m.: McCarthy enters the monitoring room.

8:15 a.m.: Alarm sounds on a stairwell leading to the sub-basement level.

9:05 a.m.: McCarthy enters the monitoring room.

9:06 a.m.: Mankoff enters the monitoring room.

9:07 a.m.: McCullom enters monitoring room.

9:09 a.m.: Guard Todd Wilson enters the United Bank Center building and gains access to the building containing the cash vault and monitoring area.

9:14 a.m.: McCullom dispatched to lower level to admit man who called identifying himself as a vice president. Authorities believe McCullom was killed then.

9:20 a.m.: Alarm sounds on the stairwell.

9:24 a.m.: McCullom's access card used to enter monitoring room.

9:26 a.m.: Wilson enters the monitoring room. Authorities believe all three guards were killed by this point.

9:33 a.m.: Someone in monitoring room resets alarm on records tunnel.

9:48 a.m.: McCullom's access card used to enter the cash vault.

9:56 a.m.: McCullom's access card used to exit the cash vault.

The Gazette Telegraph, 1992
Bibliography

American Optometric Association, 2019

Associated Press, 1991, 1992

Boulder Daily Camera, 1991, 1992

Colorado Springs Gazette Telegraph, 1991, 1992, 2001

Cutler, Brian L. (edited by), Expert Testimony on the Psychology of Eyewitness Identification, American Psychology Law Society Series, 2009, Oxford University Press, New York, New York

The Daily Sentinel, 1991, 1992

Denver Post, 1991, 1992, 2001, 2013

Gerash, G.L., & Goodstein, Phil, "Murders in the Bank Vault, The Father's Day Massacre and the Trial of James King", Denver New Social Publications, 1997, Denver, Colorado

Lexis Advanced, n.d.

Parabon Nano-labs

People Magazine, "Bloody Sunday", Arias, Ron, August, 1991

Reuters Wire, 1991, 1992

Rocky Mountain News, 1991, 1992, 2001

Wikipedia, Father's Day Bank Massacre, n.d.

Wikipedia, Parabon Nano-labs, 2019

IN MEMORANDUM

In Memorandum

I called Judge Spriggs in March and left him a voicemail. I wanted to interview Judge Richard T. "Dick" Spriggs for my book. I knew it was a long-shot. Judges don't often participate in interviews. Judge Spriggs died while I was writing the book on October 21, 2019. He was born in Rome, New York, in 1935. Judge Spriggs had a 50-year-long career as a lawyer and a judge in Denver, Colorado. He retired as a judge in 1999. His other passion was fly-fishing. Watching him on tape, he was a character with a little bit of temper but a good sense of humor. He was a no-nonsense judge. His personality and knowledge of the law were large enough to counter all of the strong personalities in the courtroom. I wish I would have had the opportunity to talk with him. Judge Spriggs was 84-years-old. Rest in Peace, Judge Spriggs.
https://horancares.com/obits/richard-t-dick-spriggs/

In Memorandum

Courtesy, Court TV, 1992

ABOUT THE AUTHOR

Kimberli lives near Denver, Colorado
with her husband and two Boston
Bull Terriers. They have two adult
children. She is currently working on her
PhD in Public Policy and the Law.

Kimberli was born in Charleston, West Virginia in 1967.
She is a proud graduate of Marshall University
with a Degree in Print Journalism and a Minor in Polit-
ical Science.
Kimberli moved to Colorado in 1990. She received a
Master's Degree
in Public Policy in 2011. She has written two other books:
"Sleeping in the Bathtub", 2018
"Stepping Stones to the Nightingale", 2019

Made in the USA
Coppell, TX
17 June 2021